The 3000 Questions About Myself Book for Him

The 3000 Questions About Myself Book for Him

A Questions About Me Book for Him to Explore Identity, Deepen Relationships, and Build Self-Awareness Through Bold, Meaningful Reflection

Aria Capri Publishing Group
Mauricio Vasquez
Toronto, Canada

Authors:
Aria Capri Publishing Group
Mauricio Vasquez
First Printing: May 2025

ISBN 978-1-998729-46-3 (Electronic book)
ISBN 978-1-998729-45-6 (Hardcover book)
ISBN 978-1-998729-44-9 (Paperback)

Introduction

Somewhere along the way, men were taught to have all the answers. But what if the real strength lies in asking the right questions?

In a world that demands constant doing, it takes courage to pause, reflect, and get curious about who you are beneath the noise. *3000 Powerful Questions for Him to Reflect, Connect, and Grow* is not just a book of prompts—it's a trusted companion for men who want more from life: more clarity, more connection, more purpose.

Whether you're navigating a career transition, building stronger relationships, redefining your identity, or simply searching for space to think—this book is built for you. It's structured to guide you through honest, thoughtful exploration of your values, beliefs, habits, and dreams. No therapy-speak. No lectures. Just questions—crafted with emotional intelligence and masculine insight—to help you see yourself more clearly.

This isn't about fixing you. It's about knowing you. Because the better you understand yourself, the more intentional and powerful every area of your life becomes.

You can use these questions in whatever way serves you best:

- Solo journaling to unpack thoughts, clear your mind, or map your next move.
- Conversations with a partner to deepen emotional intimacy without pressure.
- 1:1 friendships or group settings to spark meaningful dialogue beyond small talk.

Each question is an invitation—not an interrogation. Some will be light and surprising. Others might catch you off guard—in a good way. That's the point. Growth doesn't always come from answers; it comes from *brave curiosity*.

As you move through these pages, you may uncover forgotten ambitions, new perspectives on past experiences, or even patterns you're finally ready to change. The benefits are subtle but powerful: more clarity in your decisions, stronger connections with people who matter, and a growing sense of alignment between who you are and how you live. So give yourself permission to show up honestly.

Start where you are. Go at your own pace. You don't have to prove anything to anyone. This space is for *you*—your thoughts, your story, your next chapter. Because asking the right questions doesn't make you less of a man. It makes you a man who's awake, aware, and willing to grow. Let's begin.

How to Use This Book

- **Choose with intention:** Every question asks you to make a call—go with your gut. The goal isn't perfection—it's clarity.

- **Dig into your "why":** The answer matters, but the explanation matters more. That's where real insight and honest conversation begin.

- **Use it your way:** Start at page one or flip to wherever you feel drawn. Journal your thoughts, talk them out, or sit with them quietly. No pressure. Just presence.

- **There's no "right" answer:** This is a space for real reflection, not performance. Be honest. Be curious. Be yourself.

- **Cut the noise:** Silence the phone. Ditch the background distractions. Make space for meaningful thought and connection.

- **Let it take you off track:** If a question leads somewhere unexpected, follow it. That's often where the good stuff is hiding.

- **Keep it light when you want:** These questions aren't just deep—they're designed to bring out stories, debates, and even some laughs.

Empower Your Journey:
Discover More Tools for Success. Scan the QR Code Today

A Quick Favor to Ask

If this book has inspired reflection, sparked meaningful conversations, or brought you closer to someone in your life, I'd be incredibly grateful if you could take a moment to leave a review.

As an independent author without the resources of a big publishing house, your feedback truly makes a difference. Reviews help others discover this book, and they remind me why this work matters—one question, one reader at a time.

To share your thoughts, simply scan the QR code. It only takes a minute, but your words will go a long way.

Thank you, sincerely, for your time and support
Aria Capri Publishing

P.S. Don't miss your free bonus!
You'll find a special gift waiting for you at the **end of this book**—a digital version of *THIS IS MY WAY* you can download and keep with you wherever you go.

The 3000 Questions About Myself Book for Him

1. When was the last time something challenged what you thought you knew — like a surprising fact or a powerful conversation?

2. Would you be curious enough to explore your destiny through a psychic reading, or would you rather shape your path blindly?

3. Picture your team cheering for you — what did you accomplish that made them proud?

4. What was your latest "I need to know this now" search — and what drove it?

5. Have you ever spent a whole day in your pajamas just to relax or recover from burnout?

6. Which gemstone would symbolize your values or mindset — something strong, bold, or rare?

7. Which tale of a loyal, fearless animal has inspired you or stuck with you over time?

8. Which season feels like your natural rhythm — the one that energizes or grounds you most?

9. What's the wildest or most intense Monday you've ever survived? What made it memorable?

10. Would you protect a friend's secret if it risked another person's safety — or speak up?

11. If someone broke into your space and took one thing, what would cause the most chaos or frustration?

12. What task or goal have you been dodging, even though you know it matters?

13. Tell me about a time a joke or prank didn't land the way you thought it would — how did you handle it?

14. If you could hand off one chore for the rest of your life, what would you gladly give up?

15. Is there an old-school track that always gets you — maybe from your parents' or grandparents' era?

16. Do you have a childhood habit, like avoiding sidewalk cracks, that you've carried into adulthood?

17. What kind of wisdom, motivation, or humor would you sneak into a fortune cookie for someone to discover?

18. If you could swap two famous tough-guy leads into each other's roles, what would the results be?

19. What skill, strength, or habit have you been praised for the most over the years?

20. What are your thoughts on justice versus rehabilitation — especially for people with life sentences?

21. What character from a show you loved growing up reminds you of fun, freedom, or friendship?

22. Is there a lesser-known event in history that fascinates you or makes you pause in disbelief?

23. What moment or decision today gave you a sense of personal accomplishment — even if no one else noticed?

24. Picture your memorial bench — where would you place it to reflect your journey or passions?

25. If your favorite username became a cologne, what would it smell like — bold, earthy, fresh, mysterious?

26. If your look could launch something — a movement, a mission, a message — what would it be?

27. Who's your top pick for James Bond — and what did he bring to the role that stood out?

28. What goal did you crush even when people told you it was impossible? How did it feel?

29. Imagine a tough, masculine-sounding name for a drinking glass — what would it be?

30. If you could approach high school again, how would you show up differently as a guy?

31. What's one task, decision, or conversation you delayed for too long but finally faced?

32. Which musician would you want to perform with — and would you go for a classic, rock, or something bold?

33. Is there an old friend, mentor, or teammate you wish you'd stayed in touch with? What would you say if you met again?

34. What grooming tools or products are your go-to essentials — no matter the day?

35. What three bold, classic, or earthy colors capture who you are at your core?

36. Which animal would have the most to rant about if it could speak its mind — and what would its complaints be?

37. When it comes to Halloween, what candy makes it all worth it for you?

38. Imagine the mom version of a dad joke — what would it sound like, and would it be better or worse?

39. Can you tie a proper knot — like a square knot or a bowline — or is it time to brush up on your scout skills?

40. Imagine giving a powerful tail to an animal that doesn't usually have one — what would be cool or weird about it?

41. What's a time you seriously wished you could disappear — and how did you recover your cool?

42. Do you hang up, joke around, or listen politely when a telemarketer gets through?

43. If you had to reinvent yourself with a new name — something bold or meaningful — what would it be?

44. When was your last swim in open water, and what did it make you think or feel?

45. In your opinion, what job comes with the most impressive or powerful-looking uniform?

46. Did a coincidence or unexpected meeting ever change your direction — personally or professionally?

47. Ever walked into a meeting or date with something awful in your teeth? What was it, and who told you?

48. You open the door and find puppies — what's your action plan: rescue mission or panic?

49. Is there a word that annoys you every time you hear it? What would you happily ban forever?

50. You're handed the mic — what's your karaoke anthem that gets the room pumped?

51. Would you quietly solve a problem to protect your child's innocence, or be upfront about life's tougher lessons?

52. Do you believe there are advanced civilizations out there — and if so, how do they make you feel about humanity?

53. Which of your boyhood friendships still matter today — and how have they shaped you?

54. What youthful belief did you once defend fiercely but let go of as you grew older?

55. What gift would you pass on to a newborn to give them strength, joy, or wisdom in life?

56. Is genius about raw intelligence, or the ability to solve tough problems in unexpected ways?

57. A leak's just started in your ceiling — what's your quick fix solution in that moment?

58. If you could vanish and reappear anywhere on Earth, what place would you choose — and why?

59. What's a funny phrase you'd create to replace "until the cows come home" — maybe something with sports or action?

60. What's the most intense or surprising workout you've ever followed at home — and did it work?

61. What alternative name would you give a fly — something humorous, gross, or inventive?

62. Do you remember a time you got zapped by static — what were you wearing or walking on?

63. What was your go-to source for knowledge before the internet — libraries, magazines, mentors?

64. Are there certain harsh sounds that instantly annoy or stress you out — drills, alarms, shouting?

65. What kind of view — city, ocean, mountains, or workshop — would inspire your best focus and energy?

66. What unexpected or wild animals would you add to make animal crackers a little more adventurous?

67. If you could walk into any kitchen as a critic, what spot would you choose for bold flavors or big stories?

68. What font do you use when you want your words to look sharp, bold, or no-nonsense?

69. When's the last time you took a risk just for the thrill — like sliding down a bannister?

70. Picture this like a challenge: how many pumped-up balloons could you realistically stuff into your room?

71. What fun or purely indulgent thing would you buy right now — no justification needed?

72. What's something you tested the waters with recently — literally or in life?

73. What made you strike up a conversation with someone new — and how did it turn out?

74. Which director could turn your life into a cinematic journey, with the tone and grit it deserves?

75. What popular movie didn't live up to the hype for you — was it the plot, pacing, or just not your thing?

76. Do you carry a keychain that represents something — a place, person, or personal story?

77. Which iconic sports figure — past or present — has a face everyone would recognize?

78. What day in your life would you relive, whether to savor a victory, fix a regret, or feel alive again?

79. What's a time you got called out for bending the truth — and how did you handle the fallout?

80. Where were you the last time a rainbow appeared — did it stop you in your tracks?

81. What color would best represent a rainstorm if you had to invent a term like "whiteout"?

82. What's one thing — tool, keepsake, or symbol — that you'd jokingly or seriously call "my precious"?

83. What's your most legendary costume — something cool, hilarious, or clever you still talk about?

84. As a modern-day wizard or witch, what would replace your broomstick — a motorcycle? A drone?

85. Would you trade the use of your main thumb for total disease immunity — or is that too extreme?

86. Is there a go-to property you always aim for in Monopoly — maybe because it pays off or just feels right?

87. If you were given an investment opportunity today, where would you place your money — stocks, tech, real estate?

88. Have you ever scored a deal or rare item on eBay that made you proud or nostalgic?

89. Have you come across any unusual or fascinating methods of communication — maybe through sound, gesture, or tech?

90. What's your ultimate "guy's day" escape — whether it's adventure, solitude, or just pure fun?

91. What animal would you want to have a real conversation with — and what questions would you ask it?

92. How would you weigh loyalty, love, and compassion if faced with the difficult decision to end a pet's pain?

93. If you had to pick a place name that would be ridiculous as a celebrity baby name, what would it be?

94. What's your go-to seat on a plane for a long trip — extra legroom, quick exit, or best view?

95. What's the funniest or most intense thing you ever tried to speed-run just to see if you could?

96. When caught unprepared with a runny nose, do you tough it out, improvise, or retreat?

97. Is there a ride that brings out your thrill-seeking side or reminds you of childhood fun?

98. In a moment of unexpected isolation, what's your strategy — problem-solve, wait it out, or ask for help?

99. Which massive book did you tackle from start to finish — and was it worth the time?

100. Imagine being a genie hiding in something unexpected — where would you live and what's your summoning rule?

101. What single word captures the essence of your best buddy — loyalty, grit, or humor?

102. Would banning cars from city centers improve life or just shift the frustration elsewhere?

103. What's a time you knew you just got lucky — and avoided a mess, danger, or major setback?

104. Be honest: ever ignored a knock at the door because you weren't in the mood? Who was calling?

105. What funny or practical tools would you want instead of hands — something totally unexpected?

106. How would you describe your favorite color using three real-world things — vehicles, landscapes, or gear?

107. Would you accept cash for a selfie from a stranger, or would it raise a red flag?

108. What brutal honesty once hit you hard but ended up shaping you for the better?

109. Do you make an effort to know your neighbors — or do you prefer to keep to yourself?

110. Was there ever something written about you in school that motivated you to succeed beyond expectations?

111. Is there a "sport" you think should be called something else — more like a game or hobby?

112. If your schedule cleared for a few hours today, what would be your ideal reset or recharge activity?

113. What's the most unpleasant thing you've ever eaten by mistake — and what did you think it was?

114. Who's one actor you think doesn't have to act much — because their roles are just like them in real life?

115. What kind of legacy, courage, or boldness turns someone from memorable to legendary?

116. Which category in a quiz game is your secret strength — sports, history, or maybe pop culture?

117. Looking back, would attending college (or choosing a different path) have changed your life today?

118. What's the wildest or most hilarious tattoo typo you've come across — and could you imagine having it?

119. Imagine having to face everything head-on, never backing up. How would your day-to-day actions change?

120. Ever caught yourself drooling or dozing in public — what did you do, and who noticed?

121. If you could pick your siblings, would you go for brothers, a sisterhood of support — or fly solo?

122. Would you sacrifice a year of your life to give your loyal pet one more year with you?

123. Have you ever heard a bird make a wild or human-like sound — car alarm, chainsaw, maybe your ringtone?

124. Be honest: have you ever challenged yourself or a friend to fit as many snacks in your mouth as possible?

125. What type of volunteer work would you be proud to do — something hands-on, strategic, or inspiring?

126. Got a favorite way to describe someone who's a little slow on the uptake — but in a funny, kind way?

127. Have you ever scoped someone's social feed before a meeting or date? Who's your most recent "research"?

128. What's a big ask you've made in your life — and did it strengthen or test your bond with that person?

129. Have you come across someone with your last name who wasn't related — and did it spark curiosity or pride?

130. A stray dog shows up at your door — would you bring it in, call for help, or keep your distance?

131. Looking back at today, what are three wins, peaceful moments, or simple joys you're grateful for?

132. You're left waiting for a big interview — what's your move: stay calm, reschedule, or take charge?

133. What's your proudest (or funniest) prank — the kind you'd still brag about to close friends?

134. You've got sixty seconds to pick your dream destination — where do you go and why?

135. What would be your ideal weight or fitness level — and how would it change your confidence or energy?

136. Was there a Sesame Street character you looked up to, laughed at, or learned from most?

137. Have you ever had a "rival" — in sports, work, or life — who pushed you to be better (or more stubborn)?

138. When's the last time you gave a nod, smile, or friendly gesture to someone you didn't know?

139. What decade do you feel most connected to — for its culture, history, or spirit?

140. What kind of theme song or anthem would match the highs, lows, or humor of your day?

141. Do you know any high school sweethearts who turned their young love into a lasting marriage?

142. What dish is delicious but deadly for your stomach — the one you regret even while eating it?

143. Have you ever joined a Dungeons and Dragons game — and if not, would you want to explore that world of imagination?

144. What's a recent moment where you overreacted — even though looking back, it wasn't a big deal?

145. If someone from the past saw our world today, what part do you think would shock or disappoint them most?

146. When do you choose to be alone — to recharge, refocus, or simply enjoy your own company?

147. What's something that got lots of attention but, in your opinion, wasn't actually very good?

148. If you had to grade your daily nutrition choices, what score would you give yourself — and why?

149. What should the next generation be called — something strong, wild, hopeful, or surprising?

150. Would you trade years of your life for wealth? How much is enough to risk your time on Earth?

151. You're marooned. Who are the six people you'd pick for survival, strategy, and maybe a few laughs?

152. Ever snuck into a game, concert, or movie? What made you do it — thrill, rebellion, or pure fun?

153. If visitors from another world landed, where would you take them to show our best — the wild, the wise, or the weird?

154. How many iconic guy-girl duets can you name — across rock, country, pop, or any genre?

155. If you could dip three foods into chocolate — even wild ones — what would you dare to try?

156. You're falling, you're indestructible — what crazy stunt or landing would you pull off when you hit the ground?

157. When you're exhausted, what's the phrase you use — something tough, gritty, or a little sarcastic?

158. Would you offer a stranger a lift — trusting your gut, or playing it safe?

159. What animal would you pick as your spirit guide — something fierce, wise, or wild?

160. If you could tweak your height with a snap, would you choose to stand taller — or embrace being more compact?

161. Do you stick to a plan when you shop — hitting the aisles in a set pattern, like a secret mission?

162. Was there a trophy, badge, or ribbon from your younger years that still makes you grin today?

163. A hundred years from now, how would you want your grit, leadership, or humor to be remembered?

164. Which athlete's cheating scandal still bothers you — the one that broke trust for fans?

165. What unlikely actor would turn Indiana Jones into a comedy instead of an adventure?

166. If you had to bet on your expert knowledge for a trivia contest, what subject would you crush?

167. What traits — passion, obsession, knowledge — do you think define a nerd in the best way?

168. What's your worst "it looked better in the photos" moment from staying in a hotel?

169. Would you confront, report, or ignore a coworker you caught stealing — and how would you weigh your options?

170. Was there ever a moment when you shared a bath, either from romance, childhood, or pure convenience?

171. When have you chosen caution over risk — and did it pay off or feel frustrating?

172. What single word could you yell in public that would create instant confusion or panic?

173. If your ship finally came in, what treasures — success, freedom, family — would it bring?

174. What's your nightly shutdown routine — the last thing you do to get ready for sleep?

175. You're setting sail on a free two-week cruise — who's your ultimate partner-in-adventure?

176. If billions of people jumped together at once, what effects would you predict — physically or metaphorically?

177. How well do you know your remote — or do you mostly stick to volume, power, and channels like most people?

178. What's your favorite tone of beige — and if you had to brand it with a bold or funny name, what would it be?

179. If a new Musketeer joined the team, what strong, fearless, or funny name would fit them best?

180. Was there ever a moment when you shared a bath, either from romance, childhood, or pure convenience?

181. When have you chosen caution over risk — and did it pay off or feel frustrating?

182. What single word could you yell in public that would create instant confusion or panic?

183. If your ship finally came in, what treasures — success, freedom, family — would it bring?

184. What's your nightly shutdown routine — the last thing you do to get ready for sleep?

185. You're setting sail on a free two-week cruise — who's your ultimate partner-in-adventure?

186. If billions of people jumped together at once, what effects would you predict — physically or metaphorically?

187. How well do you know your remote — or do you mostly stick to volume, power, and channels like most people?

188. What's your favorite tone of beige — and if you had to brand it with a bold or funny name, what would it be?

189. If a new Musketeer joined the team, what strong, fearless, or funny name would fit them best?

190. Should breakdancing be recognized on the world stage like boxing or basketball? What's your take?

191. Have you come across a strange or hilarious scientific name that stuck with you?

192. When was the last time you wondered if you were going totally crazy — and what caused it?

193. If you had to give your buddies some "most likely to..." titles, what would they be?

194. What kind of knowledge would you add to your life to sharpen your edge or fuel your passion?

195. Ever had a total disaster trying on clothes — broken zippers, wrong sizes, awkward moments?

196. Who would you secretly (and playfully) haunt if you became a ghost — just to mess with them?

197. What detail, habit, or relationship could use a little more of your focus these days?

198. Imagine a wild version of Area 51 — what secret tech, aliens, or mysteries would be hiding there?

199. Would you be willing to go bald if it meant raising serious money for a charity you believe in?

200. Do you avoid walking under ladders as a nod to tradition, safety, or just habit?

201. What's the wildest storm you've ever faced — lightning, rain, winds — and how did you react?

202. What three hearty or satisfying foods are your top picks for a no-fail picnic?

203. If every job paid the same, would you still do what you do now — or pick something bold and different?

204. Ever hurt yourself doing something totally ridiculous or minor — what's your most embarrassing injury?

205. Be honest: have you ever helped a buddy, brother, or girlfriend with a pimple situation?

206. What was the last situation — fear, frustration, or joy — that made you shout or yell out loud?

207. In your story, what everyday item would be the unexpected key to defeating an unstoppable hero?

208. Which task — tough, boring, or messy — would you hate having to tackle solo?

209. Which national parks have you trekked through, and what's one that still calls you back?

210. What's your preferred way to back up important data — cloud storage, hard drives, or something else?

211. Imagine Alice falling into another universe — what quirky, daring, or dangerous characters would she find?

212. What event or decision first made you feel like you had crossed from youth into adulthood?

213. What upgrades would you make to your car — speed, tech, off-road survival? Dream big!

214. In your view, is anyone truly irreplaceable at work — or is everyone just part of a bigger machine?

215. Alone at night — what noise would set off every alarm in your mind, even if it's just the wind?

216. When's the last time you crashed in a sleeping bag — camping, traveling, or even in your living room?

217. What's one scent you absolutely can't handle — something that flips your stomach instantly?

218. Imagine yourself as a huge gnome — what strong, bold, or hilarious pose would you be frozen in?

219. Which Scooby-Doo character matches your vibe — bold Fred, chill Shaggy, smart Velma, or someone else?

220. Be honest: what dance score (out of 10) would your buddies give you — and would you agree?

221. How many people on your friend list do you hang out with in real life — beyond just liking their posts?

222. What's your go-to "just in case" item — a tool, gadget, or gear you'd never leave home without?

223. Imagine waking up as the hero (or villain) of the last show you watched — who are you now?

224. What's your favorite Disney movie — or why do you think Disney films don't really click with you?

225. If you had to step up and lead, what mission, team, or goal would fire you up the most?

226. What's your favorite non-dairy milk — something rugged like oat milk, smooth like almond, or new and trendy?

227. Thanksgiving feast time: would you reach for a hearty savory pie or a rich sweet pie first?

228. What's the next logical step in tech evolution — after laptops and palmtops — that would fit into your life?

229. Is forgiveness real without forgetting — or do you think real strength is remembering and forgiving anyway?

230. Imagine Earth as one country. What city would you choose to represent its strength, history, or future?

231. What's the most physically demanding thing you've ever tackled — work, sport, or survival?

232. If you were out in survival mode, would you eat squirrel meat without hesitation — or hesitate?

233. Would you choose the pride of a $75,000 luxury ride or the flexibility of $50,000 in cash?

234. How much TV time do you rack up in a typical week — more than you'd like to admit?

235. Have you ever proudly or playfully dressed in the national costume of a different country?

236. Knowing your best buddy, what three things would he wish for — success, freedom, fun?

237. What heavy-hitting, high-calorie snack would you rely on to power you through a tough mountain trek?

238. Is there an amount of money that would make you willing to gain and maintain a hundred pounds for a year?

239. Are there flavors — herbs or spices — you always ditch from recipes because they just don't suit your taste?

240. What's the weirdest or most uncomfortable thing you've accidentally planted yourself on?

241. Blindfolded pin drop: what place would you dread getting stuck with for a surprise visit?

242. What new word recently made it into your conversations — and what does it mean to you now?

243. What powerful or meaningful symbols would you add to a family crest if you designed one today?

244. What's one slow-motion video that completely grabbed your attention — and why?

245. Which actor do you feel has been boxed into a certain role over and over again?

246. What's your dream breakfast lineup — hearty, fast, luxurious, or comforting?

247. What insect would you pick to become if you had to — strong like an ant, agile like a dragonfly?

248. Imagine getting rushed to the ER — what ridiculous thing would you NOT want to be caught wearing?

249. How big is your social media circle — and do you actually keep up with everyone you follow?

250. What bold or surprising cotton candy flavor would you love to create for adventurous taste buds?

251. When's the last time you balanced up and down on a seesaw — and who was with you?

252. What's the most surprising or unusual custom from another culture that made you stop and think?

253. Power's out — what's your plan to stay calm, safe, or even entertained when everything goes dark?

254. In which areas of life are you willing to settle — and where do you push for excellence?

255. What trio of ingredients do you trust to make a smoothie that fuels you and satisfies your cravings?

256. What's another food so good you'd happily get your hands messy for it?

257. What ultimate music fest would you pick to experience live — rugged camping or big city stages?

258. As a daring high-dive champ, what bold or crazy move would you create — and how would you name it?

259. What sci-fi film feels scarily close to where you think life on Earth is actually heading?

260. Which modern tech device would look awesome if reworked into a rugged steampunk machine?

261. When's the last time you tossed a frisbee around — who was with you, and where did it happen?

262. What cookie pairs best with milk for you — classic, chunky, or homemade?

263. If everyone could read your unfiltered thoughts today, would you be apologizing left and right?

264. What's that classic story your family always brings up that gets a laugh at your expense?

265. When did a moment of total silence feel so powerful it was almost louder than noise?

266. When you're packing up to leave for a trip, what's your last must-do ritual or checklist item?

267. If you could move your birthday for a strategic reason (better weather, fewer obligations), what new day would you choose?

268. What old toy have you kept from childhood — maybe tucked away, displayed, or handed down?

269. Picture yourself trapped in a rising tunnel — what clever tools or tricks would you invent to escape?

270. Have you ever met someone with a name that made you do a double-take — or laugh out loud?

271. Would you eat packaged food that's technically expired — or is that a hard no for you?

272. Spill emergency! What's your move if red wine hits a white carpet — action, denial, or calling for backup?

273. What one-word spell would you invent — something powerful, funny, or uniquely yours?

274. What wild twist would you invent for a plane ride — sharks, robots, pranksters?

275. If your last meal was immortalized as art, what bold or hilarious name would you slap on it?

276. Ever catch a glimpse of a face in a wall, cloud, or tree — and think, "That looks like a celebrity"?

277. How would you rename Velma, Daphne, and Fred to fit today's world — cooler, tougher, or trendier?

278. Did the tooth fairy ever visit you when you lost a tooth — and was it magic or just money under the pillow?

279. Looking back, what unexpected twist or dream come true changed your path?

280. When was your last moment of true, deep silence — and did it bring peace or discomfort?

281. What new, funny, or bold name would you give Alvin the chipmunk if you could?

282. Imagine losing one sense for a day — which would you handle best, and what would you miss most?

283. What solo game or challenge do you enjoy most — whether it's brainy, strategic, or active?

284. Have you ever felt tempted to sneak a look at someone's private notes or journal — and did you?

285. What's the last moment you froze in a photo — something real, beautiful, funny — that wasn't about you?

286. What dream skill would you love to completely master — whether it's physical, mental, or creative?

287. Ever played a wild game of piñata smashing? What's your most epic hit (or hilarious miss)?

288. Should there be a strict rule to hold off all Christmas celebrations until December 1st?

289. What's something simple that you keep forgetting — even though you swear next time you won't?

290. How often do you give out hugs during your day — and who's usually on the receiving end?

291. What new name would you invent for an orange — something bold, funny, or clever?

292. Are you the type to sip iced coffee even during a snowstorm — or do you change with the season?

293. Which Eastwood classic do you admire — or do you find yourself unmoved by his style?

294. As a landscape artist, what natural scene — rugged, wild, or peaceful — would you want to paint first?

295. What's the most rugged, surprising, or skillful thing you've seen someone accomplish with just their feet?

296. Which space at home is your personal headquarters — where you spend the most hours?

297. What day would you push off to once every four years — to skip hassle, pressure, or annoyance?

298. What trio of artists would you love to see rock a stage together — legendary, unexpected, or dreamlike?

299. Based on everything you already know, what PhD would you be awarded today without extra study?

300. What food had you fooled with its looks — only to totally let you down when you tasted it?

301. Be honest: have you ever faked a homemade cake moment by buying it from a store?

302. Imagine reinventing "on a rope" products — what modern item would you attach for laughs or convenience?

303. What's that look you give — at work or at home — that everyone understands instantly?

304. If your name became an acronym, what bold, rugged, or cool traits would the letters stand for?

305. If disaster struck, what place would be the most dangerous, embarrassing, or frustrating to have a heart attack?

306. What color instantly reminds you of festive seasons, big celebrations, or family traditions?

307. Have you ever built a backup stash of essentials — just to be ready for the unexpected?

308. If pandas weren't black and white, what cool or wild color combinations would you want to see instead?

309. Imagine building a massive creation seen from outer space — what design would you go for?

310. What's one food that should never come out of a can or freezer — fresh only, or not at all?

311. Do you buy into the idea that nothing is impossible — or are you more grounded about certain realities?

312. Could you stomach eating a beetle if your pride (or prize money) was on the line?

313. In today's world, what clever thing would Hansel and Gretel scatter to find their way back?

314. What's your dream recipe for the most epic ice cream float ever — flavors and fizzy drinks included?

315. Have you ever faced a heartbreak that changed you — and what did you learn from it?

316. What's a little thing people do that just gets under your skin no matter how small it is?

317. Can you think of a recent moment when everything went wrong and you just shook your head at your luck?

318. Imagine high stakes: could you rattle off the alphabet backwards in half a minute — or totally choke?

319. What ridiculous but believable excuse could you invent if you were late — and actually get away with it?

320. What do you think it takes for a long-distance relationship to survive the miles and the challenges?

321. If you could skip dishwashing by eating your plate, what flavor would make it totally worth it?

322. You left your lunch at home. Would you tough it out, grab fast food, or hunt for a quick fix?

323. What color trend do you think has faded — and do you still rock it anyway?

324. Outside of lemonade, what's your favorite thing to whip up with fresh lemons?

325. What holiday song makes you groan when it starts playing everywhere?

326. What sport would you bravely or awkwardly compete in if you had to step up for your country tomorrow?

327. Looking back, what did you fight hard to defend that now makes you shake your head and laugh?

328. What ravioli stuffing — hearty, cheesy, or bold — do you crave the most?

329. What noise — a crack of a bat, a lawn mower, a splash — brings summer rushing back for you?

330. What small, unexpected gesture of kindness made a bigger impact on you than you realized at the time?

331. What was the last funny, serious, or random question you threw at your smart speaker?

332. What fresh, hearty, or nostalgic things do you love picking up at a local farmers market?

333. What first job best teaches teens about grit, patience, and earning a paycheck?

334. Pick three words that best describe how your day is shaping up right now — no explanations needed.

335. What luxury, treat, or indulgence would you love to dive into and stay buried in for a while?

336. The media wants a soundbite about your work — how would you prepare or dodge the spotlight?

337. With just old newspapers, what inventive, rugged, or funny project would you craft?

338. In a pinch, who's the one person you trust most to have your back without question?

339. Which historical wonder would you mourn the most if it was lost to time or disaster?

340. What breaking news headline would you love to be the first to deliver behind the anchor desk?

341. If you could rewrite Little Red Riding Hood, how would you flip the story's ending on its head?

342. Have you ever felt protected or inspired by something you believed could be an angel?

343. What's the most awful combination of leftovers you could imagine being thrown into a pie?

344. Based on your attitude, what playful nickname would your friends jokingly (or lovingly) give you?

345. What legendary movie prop would you proudly display — a sword, a jacket, a vehicle?

346. When's the last time you tackled a feast so big you needed a full-on food recovery nap?

347. What three wins — small victories or joys — are giving you reasons to smile today?

348. How often do you meet people with your same first name — and does it feel funny or familiar?

349. When's the last time you felt genuinely impressed and said, "That's cool!" out loud?

350. What legendary beast would you want to see walking (or flying) around in real life?

351. Where's your top choice for grabbing a great meal in your town if visitors asked for a recommendation?

352. Have you ever eaten something you didn't recognize — maybe on a dare, an adventure, or just curiosity?

353. Which strange or outrageous cult story sticks in your mind the most?

354. How would you silently show your anger — with a look, a gesture, or a strong body move?

355. Do you use military time (24-hour clocks) at home, or do you stick with AM and PM?

356. What's the most "fail-proof" thing you still managed to find confusing or tricky?

357. What's the one frosting you could eat by the spoonful — chocolate, buttercream, or something wild?

358. When's the last time you truly celebrated big — maybe like it was "1999" or another special moment?

359. What's the smallest living creature or natural wonder you've ever spotted outdoors?

360. If you came up with an industrial-strength glue, what bold or rugged name would you brand it with?

361. What would you rename Butch Cassidy and the Sundance Kid if you gave them a modern or wild twist?

362. If you had a magic switch to skip one chore forever, which never-ending task would you eliminate?

363. What familiar smells bring you peace — maybe freshly cut wood, leather, or a forest after rain?

364. Based on the celebrations and farewells you've seen, what would the title of your life movie be?

365. Was there a storybook villain or creature that used to spook you as a kid?

366. In a 21st-century twist on the "Twelve Days of Christmas," what new hilarious or awesome gifts would appear?

367. What's your go-to radio station when you're on the road or kicking back at home?

368. What's the funniest or most creative name you've heard for private parts — your own or someone else's?

369. Imagine your umbrella flies away — how much effort would you realistically spend trying to catch it?

370. If you had to barter at lunch, how many fries would you demand for one good nugget?

371. Which older celebrity do you think is rocking their looks even better now than back in their prime?

372. If you could redesign baboon bottoms with a different color, what bold new choice would you make?

373. Have you wrestled with packaging that claimed to be "easy" but felt like a challenge?

374. What recently gave you an itch attack — something outdoors, at work, or even at home?

375. When it comes to pies, which one stands above all the others for you?

376. What's your idea of a perfectly sharp or classic wedding outfit that turns heads?

377. Have you ever crossed paths with someone who could've passed as your double?

378. What other names do you use instead of "thingamajig" when you can't quite remember the real word?

379. Should museums keep displaying ancient remains, or is it more respectful to send them back home?

380. If bubble gum wasn't sweet, what bold, salty, or spicy flavor would you want to chew?

381. What's the most moving or heartbreaking grave marker you've ever come across?

382. What recent moment made you genuinely mutter, "Man, that sucks," and what was the situation?

383. What's the weirdest sport or competition you've tried — either for fun or by accident?

384. If forced to delete all but three photos, which memories would you hold onto without question?

385. What are your go-to songs for belting out like a rockstar when no one's listening?

386. What podcast are you currently following — business, true crime, adventure, or comedy?

387. What high-energy songs do you blast when you need to push yourself and get things moving?

388. Would you call yourself a grinder, a go-getter, or a builder — and what are you building right now?

389. Which Springsteen song gets you fired up — or do you not vibe with his style at all?

390. As pirate captain, what strong, fearsome, or funny name would you give your ship?

391. Which subject from school surprised you by actually being useful in everyday situations?

392. If you could grow anything useful or awesome on a tree, what would you pick (besides money)?

393. What's the absolute worst place you can imagine getting a boil — physically or socially?

394. What's the most bizarre phobia you've come across — and did it make you curious or sympathetic?

395. Imagine Buddy Holly's career kept soaring — what cool or heartfelt song title might he have written next?

396. What parental warning did you shrug off as a kid but later realize was actually wise?

397. What candy would you happily munch on for life if you had an unlimited stash?

398. What embarrassing or gross thing could ruin your morning while brushing your teeth?

399. What qualification — practical, impressive, or just fun — would you wish into your pocket today?

400. Can you remember a moment you thought, "If only I were older" — and what made you feel that way?

401. What's the one car color you'd never choose — no matter how cool the car itself was?

402. What rugged or futuristic energy source would you invent — and what bold name would you slap on it?

403. What's the last silly moment that made you unexpectedly emotional — and how did you laugh about it later?

404. After a century-long sleep, what major changes would leave you amazed or confused?

405. What decision did you leave up to fate with a coin toss — and what were the two choices?

406. Do you power through every book you start, or are you willing to abandon it if it's not grabbing you halfway?

407. If you could rename a famous movie to fit its real spirit better, which one would you pick and what title?

408. If your buddies needed to find you in a bookstore, what aisle would they check first — adventure, history, tech?

409. What's the worst comment someone could make when you're fresh out of a breakup?

410. What creature do you believe rules as the deadliest on Earth — fierce, silent, or surprising?

411. What type of theme park would you love to design — action-packed, adventurous, or something wild?

412. Which animated character would totally dominate a rap battle — skills, style, and swagger combined?

413. In 10,000 years, what dramatic changes do you think Earth — and human life — will have gone through?

414. Who do you honestly find it tough to feel sorry for, even if you know you should?

415. What's the funniest or most desperate time you cleaned by cramming stuff into a hidden space?

416. Can you remember a moment you faced a challenge head-on, saying "Bring it on!" without hesitation?

417. What hilarious or bold words would you secretly paint under your boat for a good laugh?

418. What unique or outrageous Monopoly version would you create to make the game even better?

419. What's the worst case of buyer's remorse you've had — that one thing you wished you hadn't bought?

420. What's the most ridiculous or awkward kind of drive-thru you could picture being invented?

421. What snacks, drinks, or meals would you race to grab first if your shopping cart was free?

422. What's the strangest thing you've ever stuck between pages when you didn't have a real bookmark?

423. What's a recent moment you acted selfishly — whether for survival, pride, or pure impulse?

424. What's the funniest real or ironic name-job combo you've ever come across?

425. Which gum brand wins for flavor, toughness, or just plain habit in your book?

426. If you were a salad dressing, would you be bold and spicy, rich and creamy, or light and refreshing?

427. What funny moment, show, or person made you literally laugh out loud most recently?

428. What's the one piece of jewelry you never leave home without — a ring, chain, or lucky charm?

429. What item, if offered with a "buy one, get one free," would make you just roll your eyes?

430. How bad is your passport photo, really — be honest, scale of 1 to 10?

431. What's the weirdest museum exhibit you've seen — something that made you do a double take?

432. If nobody was around, how differently (or crazier) would you dance compared to when people are watching?

433. Would you match your cat to your couch if cats came in all colors — or pick the coolest color just because?

434. Disaster strikes: the toilet won't flush — how would you handle it without total embarrassment?

435. When was your last adventure roasting marshmallows — a campfire, beach, or backyard?

436. If the Olympics were hosted by your city, what strong, funny, or proud mascot would you create?

437. What disastrous bedroom color scheme would be your nightmare if a TV makeover show took over?

438. What decade's vibe — style, music, spirit — would you love to experience as a teenager?

439. If you were a Power Ranger, what color would best match your personality and style?

440. Quick challenge: how many European capitals can you name without pausing to Google?

441. Imagine a pop star fronting a hardcore metal band — who would be the most hilariously wrong pick?

442. What skill or craft would you sign up to learn right now if time and money didn't matter?

443. Imagine your vibe turned into a smell — rugged, fresh, musky, or wild — what would it be?

444. What teenage blunder makes you chuckle (or wince) the most now when you think about it?

445. What tough, bold, or hilarious items would you choose as game pieces if you invented a board game?

446. What are the three timeless tracks you keep going back to, no matter what?

447. How else could you put a table tennis ball to use — maybe in DIY hacks, pranks, or games?

448. Which bold, charming, or hilarious male actors would you pick to form a guy version of Charlie's Angels?

449. What separates surviving from thriving in your life — what keeps you fully alive?

450. When was the last time déjà vu hit you — and did it leave you amazed, confused, or both?

451. What bold or funny bowling team name would you and your crew proudly wear on your shirts?

452. Imagine colorful cobwebs hanging around — would you leave them up as wild art or still clear them out?

453. What ancient part of nature — rock, river, forest — have you seen that left you in awe?

454. When's the last time you showed toughness on the outside even when you felt crushed inside?

455. What's the last place you shopped where the service was so good it stuck with you — and what were you buying?

456. Which sports team would you love to cheer for live all season if you had free tickets?

457. What's your go-to board game when you want to challenge yourself or bond with friends?

458. Are you the type who powers through New Year's resolutions, or do they quietly disappear?

459. Would you consider cryogenic freezing to see the world a hundred years from now — or does it freak you out?

460. Can you name a few people you personally know whose names start with B — like Brian, Beth, or Ben?

461. What's your proudest sale win — a big-ticket item or an unexpected gem?

462. Imagine cockroaches had voices — deep and gruff, or high and sneaky — what do you think they'd say?

463. What's the most hilariously bad or frustrating parking fail you've seen — and where did it happen?

464. Only one bread for life — hearty rye, fluffy white, warm naan — what's your choice?

465. What's the smoothest or luckiest paycheck you've ever pulled in without breaking a sweat?

466. Who would you honor with a loud, proud radio shout-out if you had 10 seconds of air time?

467. Where's the strangest room you've found yourself — abandoned, colorful, mysterious — and why?

468. Should animals have legal rights similar to humans — dignity, freedom, protection — or is that unrealistic?

469. In a new Wizard of Oz remake, what updated footwear would Dorothy rock — sneakers, boots, tech shoes?

470. What moment recently left you speechless or seriously impressed enough to say, "Wow!"?

471. Which planet would you love to explore — from its wild storms to its mysterious landscapes?

472. What's the strangest piece of gear, tool, or just plain odd thing you keep in your car?

473. Can you proudly (or shamefully) say you've won a burping contest — or at least entered one?

474. Which optical illusion completely blew your mind when you first saw it — and why?

475. Imagine dinosaurs returned — what modern place would be perfect for them to roam safely?

476. Can you recall the words to "Frère Jacques," or do you just hum the tune when it pops into your head?

477. What topic in general knowledge quizzes always seems to leave you stumped?

478. What's your best move when you go for a high-five and get left hanging — own it or laugh it off?

479. When did you assume someone was bluffing or joking, but they were actually being completely honest?

480. If you could redesign black holes to look less intimidating, what bold color would you pick?

481. How many things in your house beep at you — and which one drives you the most crazy?

482. What's the thing you do that's probably the most wasteful — even if you know better?

483. What dance best captures the rhythm of your week so far — smooth, clumsy, or full of energy?

484. What's your most practical app — and what's the guilty pleasure app you still keep for fun?

485. What's step one in your master plan if world domination was the goal?

486. What ridiculous superpower would make a hero totally impressive... and totally useless?

487. If Velcro retired tomorrow, what rough-and-ready replacement fastener would you design?

488. Which ABBA hit gets stuck in your head the most — and can you sing it word for word?

489. Have you ever spelled something hilarious in alphabet pasta — and when was the last time?

490. Imagine you scored ten tickets to something epic — what would it be, and which people would you want by your side?

491. If you were building the ultimate treehouse, what three awesome things would you absolutely need?

492. What's the longest you've ever waited in line — and what were you determined to buy?

493. Can you remember the last time you confidently pushed a pull-only door — and how did you recover?

494. What's a low-key awesome website you've discovered — something useful, hilarious, or surprising?

495. If you could rock any crazy hair color for a day without judgment, what wild color would you try?

496. Which couple you know has stayed married the longest — and what lessons do you think they can teach?

497. Would you proudly burn a burger-scented candle in your home — or does that sound horrifying?

498. What modern outfit would The King of Rock 'n' Roll be wearing if he walked down the street today?

499. What's a hilarious, innocent comment you heard from a child that still makes you laugh?

500. What classic or funny dance move from the past do you still remember how to do?

501. What's the funniest or craziest story you've heard about someone misusing super glue?

502. Have you ever seen (or felt) how a full moon can seem to change moods, energy, or even luck?

503. What major threat — environmental, technological, or social — worries you most for the future?

504. Would you or someone you know ever dream of driving the iconic Wienermobile?

505. Where would you most love to camp out and fall asleep under a sky full of stars?

506. What's your best (or worst) food fight story — whether you started it or just got splattered?

507. What's the oddest or funniest thing you've stumbled upon unexpectedly?

508. As a secret agent, what tough or clever code name would you proudly use?

509. What fiery natural wonder — lava, desert heat, wildfire — have you personally experienced?

510. What's your go-to "Did you know?" fact to drop when you want to sound clever or funny?

511. What funny or dramatic new word would you create to describe dragging yourself into Monday?

512. What bold, strong, or unique design would you pick for your ideal front door?

513. What song would you want every person around the globe to know and sing — at games, parties, or just for fun?

514. What's something daring, funny, or bold you did purely to win someone else's admiration?

515. What's the craziest or most regrettable tattoo you've ever seen — and where was it?

516. When and where did you last feel so relaxed that all your stress melted away?

517. What's the laziest, most brilliantly effortless thing you've ever done?

518. If photographers swarmed you thinking you were a star, who would they confuse you with — and would you play along?

519. What color would make a tempting red button seem less exciting and easier to resist pressing?

520. If you could give an awesome title to a boring chore, what would you call it to make it sound epic?

521. What event, headline, or surprise recently grabbed your focus and made you stop in your tracks?

522. Do you enjoy your own company when you're alone — or do you prefer to always be around people?

523. What profession do you see as the ultimate test of risk, bravery, or endurance?

524. If you could put an insurance policy on your strongest or most important body part, what would it be?

525. Have you ever been inside a weirdly designed building — what made it stand out to you?

526. What invention's first unveiling would you most love to witness in real time — the car, the airplane, the internet?

527. What are three skills, strengths, or talents you have that you know you can count on?

528. Would you drink from your dog's bowl if you were desperate enough — or would you stubbornly refuse?

529. What overheard comment, conversation, or moment made you laugh or raise an eyebrow recently?

530. When did you last sit down to polish your shoes — and was it for an important occasion or just habit?

531. What's a funny or memorable saying you use to describe persistence or frustration?

532. How would you rate your handwriting on a scale from barely readable to beautifully artistic?

533. What ingredients — intensity, creativity, freedom — make the perfect workout session for you?

534. Can you or anyone in your family curl their tongue — and is it considered a special talent?

535. What hilarious or overly dramatic country song title sticks out in your memory?

536. Would you jump at the chance to ride in a self-driving car — or would you need a little convincing first?

537. Where would you place a full set of armor in your home — to impress, scare, or entertain guests?

538. What's the funniest or most unexpectedly awesome little gift you ever found inside a Christmas cracker?

539. What's the funniest or most awkward place you accidentally fell asleep?

540. How often do you keep up with the news — and what story made you pause today?

541. What hilarious or outrageous cat name made you laugh the most?

542. If you had to choose one kind of floor for your whole house — hardwood, carpet, tile — what would it be?

543. What's the creepiest or funniest ghost story you've told (or heard) while sitting around a fire?

544. Can you think of a moment when you said or did something that might not have been totally PC — even if it was harmless?

545. How would you teach someone, step-by-step, to make a solid cup of tea without confusing them?

546. If you could strengthen one sense to superhero levels, which one would you boost?

547. Ever heard of anyone trying to "capture" a fart in a jar — and what's your honest opinion about it?

548. If you had to draw something at this moment, what would you doodle first — a car, a face, a dream?

549. What ridiculous caution sign have you seen that made you laugh and think, "Really? That needed a sign?"

550. How many "R" foods can you rattle off quickly — and which one's your favorite?

551. When's the last time boredom hit you hard — and what did you do to snap out of it?

552. Where would you hide your nut stash if you were a clever squirrel who didn't trust the neighbors?

553. If you could only have one kind of dip forever — salsa, guacamole, queso — which one would it be?

554. Should sports allow performance-boosting technologies — or would it ruin the spirit of competition?

555. What's the best or coolest "just add water" thing you've ever used — camping food, toys, or crafts?

556. What's one big way your approach to life differs from that of your parents?

557. What off-the-wall fitness craze would you love to create — funny, challenging, or just plain weird?

558. When the remote stops working, do you keep pressing harder — even though deep down, you know it's pointless?

559. Got a great chicken-crossing-the-road joke up your sleeve — the sillier, the better?

560. What's the most recent random act of kindness you did — big or small — that made a difference?

561. What's the weirdest or most unexpected animal you've touched — and what was it like?

562. If you had no use of your hands, could you use your creativity to get your socks on somehow?

563. Who's the biggest character you know — someone with quirks, boldness, or unforgettable charm?

564. When was the last time you couldn't help but facepalm at something ridiculous — your own or someone else's?

565. When were you last speechless — stunned, embarrassed, or just totally blank?

566. What's a topic or debate that you and your friends will probably never settle — and why?

567. Who would you choose to sit across from tonight at dinner — someone living or from history — and what would you ask them?

568. What's the craziest or most ridiculous thing you could imagine a professional news anchor accidentally saying?

569. Have you ever known someone who microwaved something weird — like socks — to warm them up?

570. If you could stuff a mattress with something completely impractical, what would it be?

571. Who would you actually trust with one of your passwords — and how many people make that list?

572. If there were no rules, what crazy "mad scientist" idea would you want to test on people?

573. What magical (or hilarious) secret formula would you imagine keeps people young forever?

574. What's a "grandpa-level" or old-school expression you still catch yourself using sometimes?

575. What's the weirdest or funniest yoga class you've ever heard about — and would you sign up?

576. If your index fingers doubled in size overnight, what hilarious challenges would you face?

577. What's a hilarious home video moment that still makes you laugh just thinking about it?

578. Would you make the heartbreaking decision to save a child at the cost of two elders if you had to?

579. Have you ever been told something totally sexist — and how did you deal with it?

580. How would you rate pumpkin pie on a scale of "absolute must-have" to "I'll pass," from 1 to 10?

581. What's a moment when you felt nervous about stepping into a room, building, or event — and why?

582. Which band would you want to rock or soothe the crowd at your farewell party?

583. What three people, moments, or gifts are you most thankful for when you really think about it?

584. Have you ever pulled the old trick of pretending to be an answering machine when picking up the phone?

585. In a big candy selection, what sweets do you always reach for first — chocolate, gummies, sour candies?

586. What type of book would capture your spirit — action-packed, heartfelt, mysterious, or hilarious?

587. If you could pick new colors for clouds floating in the sky, what wild or beautiful colors would you choose?

588. When you were little, did you ever get caught bouncing on the bed — or were you the one sneaking in jumps?

589. What's the most outrageous, crazy, or hilarious statement you've ever heard from someone?

590. Who in your family is the most likely to say or do something that leaves you cringing (or laughing) at family events?

591. Would you keep eating different foods if they all tasted exactly the same — just for the fun of it?

592. Do you secretly have a guess (serious or silly) about how your life might one day come to an end?

593. What's your most memorable experience of getting turned around or stuck in a maze?

594. Have you ever found something incredibly cool in a place where you least expected it?

595. Do you ever cheat and read the ending first when you just can't handle the suspense of a story?

596. What's the daily task that feels like it drains your energy the most — even if it's necessary?

597. Would you say "yes" to jumping out of a plane — or is skydiving just not your thing?

598. Can you remember a time when you borrowed money from someone — even for something small?

599. What's your strategy when trapped next to someone smelly in a public space — suffer, move, or joke about it?

600. What's the most creative thing you could do with a lonely glove instead of throwing it away?

601. If you had x-ray vision, what real-world advantages would it give you in work or fun?

602. Which sound — a crackling fire, a great golf shot, a soda fizz — is the most satisfying to your ears?

603. What's the biggest, toughest jigsaw you ever completed — and was it worth the struggle?

604. What strange or ridiculous accident story sticks in your mind — something you almost couldn't believe?

605. Would removing the "like" button from social media make online life less stressful for people?

606. When have you felt like the "big fish" — the standout — in a smaller group or setting?

607. What's the gift you received that made you smile awkwardly while wondering, "Why this?"

608. What's the most important tradition or feeling at the center of your Thanksgiving celebrations?

609. What typical movie scene — from dramatic reunions at airports to endless car chases — feels unrealistic to you?

610. If you could redesign the world's grass in a bold new color, what would it be?

611. Which single kitchen gadget would you fight to keep if you had to give up everything else?

612. What funny or wildly wrong explanation about where babies come from have you heard or believed?

613. Speed round: how many pink objects — real or imagined — can you name right now?

614. What's the longest jog or run you've ever completed — and how did it make you feel afterward?

615. As a daring storm chaser, what extreme weather would you love (or dare yourself) to chase?

616. What sticky situation (literally) did you last find yourself in — and what caused it?

617. What's your most memorable blind date experience — hilarious, awkward, or surprisingly good?

618. What's your gut reaction — emotionally or practically — when you encounter someone living on the streets?

619. Where would you build your perfect getaway home if you could pick any country?

620. Have you ever used a handkerchief for something creative — like a bandage, a pouch, or a mini flag?

621. When was the last time you forgot about staying dry and joyfully jumped into a puddle?

622. What creative or funny name would you pick for your own brand of premium cat food?

623. What's your top current worry — big, small, practical, or just lingering in the background?

624. Have you ever actually tried a marmalade sandwich — and would you ever eat them as much as Paddington?

625. Which teleshopping gadget made you laugh, roll your eyes, or secretly wonder if you needed it?

626. What's a time you faked not knowing something — to stay out of trouble, surprise someone, or just for fun?

627. For which items do you choose "more is better" rather than worrying about high quality?

628. Imagine gravity stopped — what's the first thing you'd hit on your way up toward the ceiling?

629. What events, dreams, or changes are you most eagerly anticipating for the rest of this year?

630. Imagine your initials were used for a "deadly virus" — what would it be called and how would it act?

631. What treasure or random surprise have you pulled out from behind or under your sofa?

632. What would be the most fun (or crazy) thing to fill a swimming pool with instead of water?

633. When was the last time you got dizzy — on purpose or by accident — and what caused it?

634. What's a bizarre or random piece of trivia you know — something you almost never get to use?

635. What would your ultimate dream house look like — how many rooms and what crazy rooms would you include?

636. If you had to pick a crayon to munch on, what color would you go for — and why?

637. Do you listen to music from your parents' generation — and if so, what songs or bands have stuck with you?

638. What's a ridiculous rule you once had to follow at school, work, or somewhere else that still makes you shake your head?

639. If you had to pick a new mascot for Greyhound buses, what animal would you choose to represent speed and travel?

640. Who's the first person you think of when you hear "can't keep a secret" — and why?

641. What's the dumbest or most hilarious mistake you've heard about someone making while committing a crime?

642. What full-size animal model would you proudly (or hilariously) display in your living room?

643. Who among your friends is most likely to create something clever that makes life easier?

644. Can you recall what you were doing during the most sweltering day you've ever experienced?

645. What undercover day job would perfectly disguise your secret life as a superhero?

646. Which part of a trifle dessert do you think steals the show: the cake, the custard, the jelly, or the cream?

647. Should famous bands stop flying around the world for concerts to be more eco-friendly?

648. What would you call a totally made-up fear of hot dogs — and how silly could you make it sound?

649. What was the best or most breathtaking thing you saw from the top of a Ferris wheel?

650. What do you think is the most unforgivable or evil crime someone could commit?

651. What type of "enclosure" would humans need in a zoo to keep them entertained and active?

652. If you could try one bold outdoor challenge — from skydiving to mountain climbing — what would it be?

653. Has anyone joked that you're a Grinch — grumpy or grumbly about holidays or happiness?

654. What group, cause, or dream would you love to lead — using your passion and ideas?

655. What dessert would you most happily devour first thing in the morning if it were allowed?

656. What's the final Christmas wish you remember making when writing to Santa?

657. What's a task or goal that seems simple on paper but tricky when you actually try it?

658. Have you ever told a lie that backfired — and what was it about?

659. Imagine your kettle could talk — what grumbles, cheers, or jokes would it make while boiling?

660. You find $20 in a hotel — do you pocket it, tell the front desk, or leave it alone?

661. If you've named your car (or anything else), what was the funniest or most meaningful name you chose?

662. Can you share your wildest or funniest story involving a giant waterslide ride?

663. Would you sacrifice an animal's life to save a person's — and would the decision haunt you?

664. What's a hilarious or playful version of "One small step for man..." that you'd announce on the moon?

665. What's a first-date comment that would immediately send everything crashing into awkwardness?

666. Did you ever have a competition (with friends or siblings) to burp the alphabet — and how did it go?

667. What do you think turns a pop song into a timeless hit — the rhythm, the hook, the story, or something else?

668. Do you focus a lot on what others think of you — or are you comfortable walking your own path?

669. What's a breakup story you've heard that was so ridiculous you almost couldn't believe it?

670. If your life depended on it, would you attempt a rooftop jump — trusting adrenaline and instincts?

671. Which accent sounds the coolest, smoothest, or most magnetic to your ears?

672. What creative new eating tool would you mash together — and what tough, cool name would you invent?

673. When did you last brew someone a cup of tea — as a gesture of friendship, comfort, or tradition?

674. Imagine you created a power-packed vegetable — what would it be called, and what super flavor would it have?

675. If you lived inside a lighthouse, what would be the hardest part — isolation, storms, or climbing all those stairs?

676. If you had to fake your own death to vanish, what daring or crazy scheme would you invent?

677. What's the most ridiculous ER trip story you've ever heard — a true "you can't make this up" moment?

678. Which friend or family member has handwriting so neat it could belong in a museum?

679. Have you ever played detective trying to catch the fridge light in the act of staying on?

680. If you were starting a gym, what bold, strong, or funny name would you choose to inspire people?

681. Is there a worn-out but beloved pair of socks in your drawer you can't quite give up yet?

682. What's a regular word you've repeated so many times that it started to sound completely ridiculous?

683. Did you ever take the elbow-licking challenge seriously — and how close did you actually get?

684. Which outrageous celebrity baby name made you do a double-take (or laugh out loud)?

685. If you could train with a world-class chef, what cuisine — hearty, spicy, traditional — would you dive into?

686. How would you style Winnie-the-Pooh today — casual, adventurous, or totally unexpected?

687. When you last felt under the weather, what knocked you off your feet — and how did you power through?

688. Among your buddies, would you be seen as the rock or the wild card — and how reliable are you, honestly?

689. What's the hardest or cleverest crossword clue you ever solved — one that made you want to high-five yourself?

690. Picnic rained out? What spontaneous indoor or rainy-day fun would you switch to?

691. What objects nearby could you MacGyver into a drum, a guitar, or a new crazy musical creation?

692. What dark, powerful, or hilariously bad-guy name would you choose if you turned supervillain?

693. From your experiences, would you say there's more kindness or cruelty in the world today?

694. What's your ultimate vacation disaster — crazy weather, missed flights, strange encounters — that became a great story later?

695. Ever sprinted up a down escalator for fun (or a challenge)? What happened next?

696. What's the most insane or jaw-dropping vehicle you've seen roaring down the highway?

697. Do you remember the last time you played leapfrog — and could you still jump like that now?

698. In case of lockdown, what's the one thing you'd make sure to stockpile — survival or pure comfort?

699. What unconscious habits — good, bad, or funny — do you often only notice afterward?

700. Who in your circle do you seriously avoid making angry — and why?

701. Have you ever treated yourself to a full day in bed — lazy, cozy, and guilt-free?

702. What's a habit, idea, or assumption you had to unlearn as you grew wiser?

703. How would you sketch your life as a line — steady climb, sudden drops, wild curves, or unexpected twists?

704. What's your go-to Starburst color — the one you secretly hope is at the bottom of the bag?

705. Are you someone who backs up your bold words with bold action — or is it something you're working on?

706. What crazy fashion trend or outfit from a catwalk made you wonder, "Who would actually wear that?"

707. Can you remember any classic jump rope rhymes from when you last played — and could you still do the moves?

708. What creative or bold alternative would you use instead of a white flag to show surrender?

709. Which noisy appliance drives you nuts when it kicks into gear — the dishwasher, the vacuum, or something else?

710. Which world leader — famous, inspiring, or controversial — would you love to share a cup of tea and conversation with?

711. What overplayed or annoying song would you erase from existence if you could?

712. As a kid, did you play "cooties" — and do you remember who you thought had them back then?

713. What food or snack recently made you so thirsty you couldn't get enough to drink afterward?

714. Looking ahead, what do you think could make you even happier than you are at this moment?

715. How many email accounts are you juggling — and which one do you like the most (or check the most)?

716. What would be a fitting (and hilarious) consequence for folks who can't return their shopping carts?

717. Have you ever tried to beat the "you can't sneeze with your eyes open" rule — and did it work?

718. What's the piece of old tech you stubbornly hold onto because it still works (or feels nostalgic)?

719. What pajamas from your childhood do you remember loving — superheroes, dinosaurs, something hilarious?

720. If your nose magically turned into a fruit, which one would you choose — something tough, bold, or funny?

721. What's the worst "I gotta go now!" moment you've ever had — and did you make it in time?

722. What's the furthest underground you've ever traveled — and how did it feel being deep below the surface?

723. What bold or funny name would you invent for your own search engine — something cooler than Google?

724. What was your all-time favorite pair of shoes — the ones you wore until they nearly fell apart?

725. What's the lowest temperature you'd willingly face before calling it quits and heading inside?

726. Which language would you love to speak fluently — for adventure, business, or pure fun?

727. If you had to rename "monkey in the middle," what crazy or cool thing would be stuck in the middle instead?

728. What's your roughest — or funniest — memory of getting queasy while on the move?

729. Do you find it easier to spot grammar or spelling errors in what others write than in your own stuff?

730. What country's customs or lifestyle would be the toughest for you personally to fully adapt to?

731. Who do you think of as a true "salt of the earth" person — solid, good-hearted, and real?

732. Would you ever trust yourself to give a friend a haircut — or have you bravely done it already?

733. Which animal's ears would you swap for yours — giant elephant ears, sneaky fox ears, or something totally different?

734. What's one memory hack, silly phrase, or acronym that really helped you nail down a tricky subject?

735. What special nicknames did you or your family use for your grandpa or grandma growing up?

736. If you could craft the ultimate frozen yogurt creation, what toppings would you pile on?

737. Imagine you were a three-course meal — what hearty, bold, or surprising dishes would you represent?

738. What items around your place could go missing, and it would take you forever to notice?

739. Can you think of a time when doing something you thought was wrong actually turned into a good thing?

740. Should society phase out fossil fuels — and if so, how quickly should it happen in your view?

741. If you could pull off a mind-blowing magic trick anytime, what trick would you love to master?

742. Are you the fiercest competitor you know — or does someone else always turn everything into a challenge?

743. What's the weirdest hiding spot where your TV remote ever ended up — under a pizza box, behind a couch, or worse?

744. Have you ever been double-dared into doing something ridiculous — and how did it turn out?

745. In your lifetime, do you think we'll see a world where hunger is finally eliminated?

746. What's the wildest or heaviest thing you've seen someone balance without dropping it?

747. In a zombie apocalypse, what's the nearest thing you could grab right now — and would it save you?

748. What delicious food would you want to magically become a spread — just to make everything tastier?

749. When's the last time you couldn't resist jumping into a big pile of raked leaves?

750. What funny or wild pattern would you create if you could leave a crop circle behind for airplanes to see?

751. What game totally hooked you so hard that you lost track of time — and do you still love it?

752. Which recent movie totally flopped for you — so bad it deserves a "worst of the year" trophy?

753. Did you ever build a CD collection — and what was the last album you proudly added to it?

754. What's a case of medical negligence that made you shake your head in disbelief?

755. What's your dream pair of designer sunglasses — tough, cool, or classic?

756. If the skies poured something other than rain, what wild thing would you imagine falling down?

757. Have you ever pretended to "get it" during a conversation — even though you were totally lost?

758. If you were building the ultimate snowman, what gear or funny items would you add?

759. You're staring down three crocodiles for a million-dollar prize. What's your strategy?

760. What's the most unexpected or strange item you've ever discovered hiding in your pocket?

761. Which of your friends or family would absolutely steal the show in a belly dancing competition?

762. Do you believe in Bigfoot — the mysterious creature of forests and legends?

763. What's the last thing you felt frustrated with yourself about — even if it was a small mistake?

764. If you could fly south for the winter like birds do, where would you head to escape the cold?

765. Besides your own birthday, what's one day you look forward to every year — and what makes it great?

766. If you could plan your last words, what powerful or funny line would you want to be remembered by?

767. If "zillion" wasn't enough, what outrageous new word would you create for an even bigger number?

768. What's the most profound or unforgettable thing someone has ever said that stuck with you?

769. If you could design the ultimate mocktail, what bold flavors would it have — and what cool name would you give it?

770. What's the angriest (and maybe most ridiculous) thing you've ever thrown during a temper flare-up?

771. Will Banksy's real name ever come out — or do you think he'll stay anonymous forever?

772. What's an example of a solution-in-search-of-a-problem product you've seen — and did you secretly want it anyway?

773. If fibbing actually set your pants on fire, would you be toasty right now — or still in good shape?

774. Have you ever felt so full of energy or mischief that you wanted to do something wild — like swinging from a chandelier?

775. When did you last go for a bike ride — and was it for adventure, exercise, or pure fun?

776. What bold or clever name would you give to a chocolate Hershey's Kiss if you had the chance?

777. If you were training to be an astronaut, what part — survival skills, fitness, or navigation — would you rock at?

778. If you had to give a quick 20-minute speech tomorrow, what topic would you totally crush?

779. Who's the YouTuber you follow most — the one whose videos you never miss?

780. On a 1–10 scale of weirdness, where do you rank — and do you wear that number with pride?

781. What onomatopoeic word — a word that makes a sound — do you love the most, and why?

782. What's your wild west cowboy (or outlaw) name — the one people would remember?

783. What's your best memory of jumping into a conga line — and where did it happen?

784. If you could order up anything — food, gear, adventure — and have it arrive now, what would you pick?

785. If you discovered a new plant in the wild, how would you describe it — and what rugged or bold name would it have?

786. When do you feel a pure, unmatched sense of bliss — like everything is just right?

787. Who among your friends has the crazy balance, patience, or silliness to spin plates like a pro?

788. Looking back, what were the top three "grown-up" things you couldn't wait to have as a kid?

789. If you could redesign Big Ben's famous sound, what bold or unexpected noise would you have it make?

790. As a Transformer, what tough or cool vehicle would you turn into — something fast, strong, or stealthy?

791. How do you burn off frustration in a strong, positive way when life gets overwhelming?

792. Could you communicate your feelings with only facial expressions and gestures — and how many different moods?

793. Is there a popular trend right now that you honestly don't understand (and maybe don't want to)?

794. How long can you hold a plank — and would you ever try pushing your limit like those endurance champions?

795. If you could step back in time for 24 hours, what exciting moment in history would you choose to witness?

796. How would you manage firing someone who's also your friend — balancing respect, loyalty, and leadership?

797. What's your best advice for handling painful muscle cramps — especially during sports or exercise?

798. Have you ever tripped over your laces like a scene from a movie — and did you laugh it off or get hurt?

799. Have you ever heard a voicemail greeting so good you wished you had thought of it first?

800. Do you have any funny or persistent habits you find hard to stop — like checking locks or tapping things?

801. Could the internet crash worldwide someday — and what crazy event would trigger it, in your view?

802. If you had to choose just one workout tool for your home, what would it be — a punching bag, a bike, or something else?

803. Have you ever idolized someone — only to later realize they're just human after all?

804. Looking at your country's shape, what object, animal, or tool does it remind you of?

805. What's the worst eating plan you ever attempted — and what lesson did you learn from it?

806. Did you ever get braces off and celebrate by doing something fun — like eating all the sticky candy you missed?

807. If you could top Shredded Wheat with anything, what would make it taste amazing and still be filling?

808. If your pet could write you a job reference, would you get hired — and what would it say about you?

809. What was the last secret Santa gift you gave — and did it go over well or lead to some laughs?

810. Have you ever been brave (or silly) enough to try twerking — and was it hilarious?

811. Deep underground at Earth's core, what's the craziest thing you could picture discovering?

812. Will we live to see a world without single-use plastics — and what bold changes would need to happen?

813. What's the funniest thing you ever climbed or balanced on when trying to grab something just out of reach?

814. What food would you jokingly slap a "danger of death" warning on because it's just that intense?

815. What's the worst moment you've had a loud stomach growl — a meeting, a date, a ceremony?

816. Should the phrase "blonde moment" disappear — and what do you think it says about assumptions?

817. What's the funniest or weirdest town or city name you've seen on a map or road trip?

818. Where were you when you last heard birds singing — and did it change your mood?

819. What scent would you choose for a powerful carpet shampoo — and what rugged or bold name would you give it?

820. What's your proudest Scrabble word — the one that made you feel like a genius?

821. Who do you know that could easily win a medal for their buffet strategy and endless appetite?

822. What's the worst thing you've stepped on without shoes — Lego? A thumbtack? Something even worse?

823. Is common sense really common — or have you seen plenty of examples that suggest otherwise?

824. What's a news event happening now that would be really tough to explain to a child without confusing or upsetting them?

825. What ridiculous drink would be hilarious to see James Bond order instead of his classic martini?

826. Who would be your ideal teammate for a three-legged race — someone fast, steady, or just hilarious?

827. What's the funniest or most awkward thing you've ever accidentally said out loud?

828. What's the most colorful or clever euphemism you've heard for taking a bathroom break?

829. You're trapped on a long flight with a crying baby next to you. What's your survival strategy?

830. Do you think people eventually get what they deserve, whether good or bad?

831. What's your best (or most disastrous) story from a buddy bonding session or team workshop?

832. As a tree, would you want to be a giant oak reaching for the sky or a sturdy tree close to the ground?

833. If you found a new galaxy, what bold or adventurous name would you want the universe to know it by?

834. What dream home improvement would you want done perfectly without lifting a finger?

835. Is there a meaningful journey you dream of taking someday — a personal pilgrimage?

836. Will technology eventually allow people to live forever — and do you think that's a good idea?

837. Have you ever tried beatboxing — and how good (or hilariously bad) was your attempt?

838. What three things come to mind when you think of Scotland — landscapes, culture, history?

839. Should top athletes step away from social media to shield themselves from racial hate — or fight back?

840. What bold, eye-catching color would you choose if your skin could change to a bright hue?

841. What's the wildest survival or daring escape story you've ever heard or read about?

842. When did you last step inside a public library — and did you find anything interesting?

843. Is there ever a situation where stealing might be understandable — like survival or justice?

844. If Jurassic Park actually existed, would you be adventurous enough to go see living dinosaurs up close?

845. What's the sneakiest or funniest example of harmless revenge you've ever come across?

846. When have you felt the unmistakable sense of being watched, even if no one was there?

847. If you needed a loyal and skilled seven-person squad for any adventure, who's on your list?

848. Are there any famous people — actors, athletes, leaders — who share your special day?

849. What's the most ridiculous car accident or insurance story you've ever come across?

850. Will brick-and-mortar stores eventually disappear because of online shopping, or will they find ways to adapt?

851. What actor do you think should have stuck to acting and left the singing to others?

852. Is school expulsion ever justified — or should there always be another way to help students?

853. What's your go-to system for organizing your schedule — digital apps, sticky notes, or old-school calendars?

854. When did you last have to swallow your pride — maybe to apologize or admit you were wrong?

855. What's the most heart-pounding or frightening event you've ever seen or experienced firsthand?

856. What's the funniest or most frustrating thing you've lost by putting it in a "safe place"?

857. If you had to go out in a blaze of glory, what epic or courageous scenario would you dream up?

858. Besides laughter, what brings you the biggest healing or happiness when you need a lift?

859. What's your go-to milkshake flavor when you need a cool, satisfying treat?

860. Would you sign up for a medical trial if the pay was good — and what's your personal "price"?

861. What's the wildest autocorrect fail that you've had to explain (or laugh about)?

862. If you absolutely had to give up a small, non-critical body part, which one would you sacrifice?

863. Have you ever had a lucky token — something you kept close during important moments?

864. What's the most recent thing you bought just because you wanted it, not because it was useful?

865. Has a bird (or any other creature) ever picked you as their unexpected bathroom target?

866. What top three websites are your first stops when you're shopping online — gear, gadgets, anything?

867. Which buddy would you jokingly never leave in charge of your home (or your dog) — and why?

868. What's one painful thing someone said to you that stuck for longer than you wished?

869. What creative, epic name would you give your ultimate candy bar mash-up of three favorite treats?

870. What's one belief or idea you absolutely reject — even if others swear it's true?

871. Was there a book you had to read for school that surprised you by how much you liked it?

872. Who would you nominate as the least likely (and maybe funniest) choice for US President?

873. When was a time you felt like nobody really got what you were trying to say or do?

874. Have you ever witnessed (or experienced) a moment when someone accidentally swallowed something crazy?

875. If Red Riding Hood had a different cloak color, what bold new color would suit her adventures?

876. Have you ever seen a garden statue, fountain, or decoration that looked seriously classy?

877. Is there a favorite cookbook you rely on when you're in the kitchen — or are you more of a freestyler?

878. What bold or unique name would you choose for a new men's cologne you designed?

879. What's the boldest last-minute decision you've made that led to an adventure (or a disaster)?

880. If the elbow's skin is called a "wenus," what would you jokingly name the skin on your nose?

881. What do you believe defines humanity — our emotions, our dreams, our creativity?

882. If you had a crystal ball for one big future question, what would you ask it to reveal?

883. When was your last all-out mud adventure — maybe from sports, hiking, or a crazy dare?

884. What's the weirdest or most unexpected Top 5 ranking you've stumbled upon?

885. If you had to switch to raw food only, what favorite hearty meals would you crave the most?

886. Where would you love to ring in the New Year with your buddies if you could pick anywhere on Earth?

887. What restaurant name made you laugh, think, or want to eat there just because it was so clever?

888. Are humans truly the peak of evolution, or do you think smarter life exists somewhere else in the universe?

889. Can you think of a time when doing the "right" thing caused more harm than good?

890. What's the worst physical or emotional pain you've experienced — and how would you rank it?

891. What's the most pointless gadget or idea you've ever seen — something that made you laugh or shake your head?

892. Have you ever had a clutch moment where you "pulled something out of the bag" and saved the situation?

893. If your last name had to be a food, what bold or adventurous one would you pick?

894. What are three things you believe cross the line so badly they're nearly unforgivable?

895. Have you ever (or would you ever) trim another person's toenails — and under what circumstances?

896. What's the snobbiest comment you've ever heard — something that made you roll your eyes?

897. If your dental implant could be any wild color, what would you choose to show off your style?

898. What product or type of thing do you hardly ever buy, even though most others seem to?

899. Looking at this week, was there a moment big enough to still matter to you a year from today?

900. What's your favorite story from a time you stayed local instead of traveling for vacation?

901. Have you ever been mistaken for someone much older or younger than you really are?

902. What's the most generous tip you've left for great service — and what made you decide to do it?

903. Which of your online usernames would actually make an awesome band name if you started a group today?

904. What home science project made you feel like a mad scientist or brought the biggest surprise?

905. Would you offer a third chance if someone let you down twice — or is two strikes enough for you?

906. What's your most epic "dead silence" or awkward moment story — when time just seemed to stop?

907. What vacation destination best matches your vibe — wild and adventurous, calm and relaxed, or somewhere else?

908. Which famous person's house, in your opinion, had the most questionable or hilarious décor choices?

909. What dream event — sports, concert, or festival — would you love VIP front-row access to?

910. What's the tallest skyscraper or lookout you've ever conquered — and was the view worth it?

911. Who's the person you know who seems to squeeze every drop out of life, chasing experiences and joy?

912. What's the most epic potato-based meal you could dream up — hearty, adventurous, or over-the-top?

913. Have you ever encountered something spooky — or do you believe in the idea of ghosts?

914. Have you ever seen a shower curtain so funny or weird it made you laugh out loud?

915. Should places like museums and theaters turn down funding from companies tied to fossil fuels?

916. Have you ever flown first class — and if you could pick any airline for the ultimate flight, which one?

917. What's the weirdest thing you've seen someone actually trying to sell?

918. What's a creative or useful app you'd love to invent — and how would it change people's lives?

919. What's the most haunting or unforgettable crime story you've ever read or heard about?

920. How many days have you pushed off doing the dishes before finally giving in?

921. What's something that really stands out to you as the ultimate example of bad manners?

922. Did you face bullying in school, and do you still remember the person who made life harder back then?

923. What's a moment when you did something super awkward simply because it was the polite thing to do?

924. Can real happiness exist without having known sadness — or are both feelings connected?

925. What bold or playful rapper name would you give yourself if you dropped an album tomorrow?

926. When do you find yourself letting discipline slide — work, fitness, hobbies?

927. What's the wildest or most controversial experiment from the past that's now banned?

928. Have you ever been seasick while traveling by boat — and what was it like?

929. What's the weirdest item you've ever bought on impulse while grocery shopping?

930. Are you someone who crushes the weekly exercise targets — or finds them tough to hit?

931. What magician's illusion totally blew your mind — one you still can't figure out?

932. As a wildlife camera operator, what incredible animal moment would you love to catch on film?

933. What's the scariest noise you've ever heard that made the hair on your neck stand up?

934. When and where did you last swim in a river — was it peaceful, cold, wild?

935. What's a question someone asked you that crossed a line and made you think, "Did they really just say that?"

936. When did you last do a double take — seeing something crazy, surprising, or funny?

937. What's a strange or awesome fact about the human body that always sticks with you?

938. Did you wear hand-me-down clothes growing up — and would you proudly thrift-shop now?

939. What's the strangest or most hilarious name for a paint color you've ever come across?

940. Who's the most effortlessly polished and sophisticated person you've ever met?

941. What's the strangest compliment someone ever gave you — one that made you laugh or scratch your head?

942. Have you ever awkwardly found out you were using the wrong name for someone — and how did you fix it?

943. When did you go the longest without a shower — maybe during a trip or adventure?

944. Which famous men do you think have the best style or coolest look?

945. What's the most daring or risky thing you've pushed yourself to do?

946. Are you still jamming to music you loved ten years ago — or has your taste totally shifted?

947. Would you be ready to help stop heavy bleeding if someone got hurt — and have you done it before?

948. Should filmmakers keep making horror movies, or has the genre run its course?

949. Is there a stubborn trait or quirky habit you have that sometimes gets in your way?

950. After hibernating all winter, what big meal would you want to eat first?

951. What was the last thing you built from a kit — and did you follow the instructions or wing it?

952. What service or item do you think should be free instead of paid — something essential or important?

953. When was the last time you used an old-fashioned map instead of relying on your phone?

954. Is there a relative whose name you're very thankful your parents decided not to pass down to you?

955. What's the most bizarre or disgusting ancient "cure" you've learned about?

956. You're short on plates at a get-together — what would you grab to serve food in a pinch?

957. What's your most epic science experiment fail from school days?

958. If you could add an extra limb — maybe for work, fun, or adventure — what would you pick?

959. If Daddy Bear, Mummy Bear, and Baby Bear had hilarious human names, what would they be?

960. Have you ever felt overwhelmed by too many choices — like at a restaurant, store, or in life?

961. What are three things you always do or have that make it finally feel like "weekend mode"?

962. When you think about how you feel inside, do you feel your real age — or totally different?

963. What's the worst hoarding situation you've ever seen or heard about — and what stood out to you?

964. What clever or funny name would you give to vegetarian bacon to make it sound appealing?

965. When was the last time you changed batteries — and what was it for?

966. Have you ever ordered something from a TV infomercial — and was it amazing or a total flop?

967. What's the most ridiculous or hilarious brand name you've seen in real life or online?

968. What board game have you swapped for an online version — and do you like it better or worse?

969. What's something — a movie, memory, or experience — that can bring tears to your eyes?

970. What bold or funny new name would you give to the "Toot Sweets" candy from the movie?

971. What's the biggest repair surprise you've faced — car, home, or something else — and how did you handle it?

972. What scene or moment on TV made you cover your eyes recently — scary, gross, or too cringey?

973. When guests are coming over, what little (or big) things do you change about your space or habits?

974. Do you play "rock, paper, scissors" with a "shoot" or just reveal your choice right away?

975. What's the worst time you ever got lost — city, countryside, or somewhere totally unexpected?

976. Where would you love to host a party that would really surprise and amaze your guests?

977. What's the most memorable or hilarious thing that happened to you at a school sports or field day?

978. Have you ever taken a daring plunge by skinny dipping — and what's the story behind it?

979. What fortune cookie message really made you smile, laugh, or think — and stuck with you?

980. Who is someone you admire for real-life bravery — a hero in your eyes?

981. Who among your friends has a laugh that's truly unforgettable — and how would you describe it?

982. What artist, album, or song have you listened to the most today — and why?

983. What two dog breeds would you mix to come up with a funny or cool new dog name?

984. What's the best or trickiest riddle you've ever heard — something you love asking others?

985. If you had to live with a noticeable scar from stitches, where would you prefer it — a badge of honor?

986. What's a film with a plot so ridiculous you had to laugh — but you still watched to the end?

987. What three sports would you combine to invent an awesome, wild, or funny new game?

988. What activity, project, or decision felt like the biggest waste of time once you were done with it?

989. Have you ever used the Forrest Gump "box of chocolates" line in real life to explain something?

990. What funny or creative word would you invent for the sizzling, bubbling sound of melting cheese?

991. What bold or clever name would you give to a new element if you found one for the periodic table?

992. If you had a magic cream that could erase one thing instantly, what would you use it on?

993. What's the most thrilling or proud moment you've had so far this year?

994. If you could have unlimited food from any restaurant or fast-food place, what would your pick be?

995. Have you ever been somewhere that felt like uncharted territory — bold, wild, and exciting?

996. What's the worst, messiest, or most ridiculous food to imagine putting between two slices of bread?

997. Is there ever a moment where stepping outside the law feels justified — or is it always dangerous?

998. If an unstoppable force met an immovable object, what do you think would happen — or what does it represent to you?

999. Would snakes seem less scary or more strange if they were covered in soft fur instead of scales?

1000. What's the most unlikely or hilarious thing a Star Wars character could say that would shock fans?

1001. How many cities beginning with "B" can you name off the top of your head — challenge yourself!

1002. You notice you received extra change at checkout — do you return it or keep it?

1003. Where would you hide 101 playful dalmatians in your house if you had to keep them secret?

1004. What ridiculous or hilarious name would you give to a new version of Harry Potter?

1005. Have you ever regifted an item — and did you get caught or was it a smooth move?

1006. What hobbies or passions do you imagine diving into after you retire?

1007. Does calling out haters make you a hater too — or is it standing up for something better?

1008. What's the coolest or most mind-blowing explosion you've ever seen in a movie?

1009. Who's a person you know who tends to overestimate their own intelligence — and makes it obvious?

1010. What was the last birthday present you bought — and was it practical, fun, or sentimental?

1011. When did having too many options leave you stuck, second-guessing, or overwhelmed?

1012. What image — a place, an object, or a feeling — could capture how you feel right now?

1013. When was your hair at its longest — and was it intentional or just something that happened?

1014. When you're under stress, what are the first changes in your behavior that give it away?

1015. If a number you don't recognize calls you, do you answer — or ignore it and hope for a text?

1016. How would you react if someone at a meal was eating with really loud, distracting noises?

1017. Where would you sneakily hide a giant cardboard cutout of The Rock in your house?

1018. Which sounds really get under your skin — something you just can't stand to hear?

1019. What's your go-to cure for hiccups — and when was the last time you had to use it?

1020. Which Monopoly playing piece do you always grab first — the car, the dog, or something else?

1021. Have you ever had an experience that made you really see life through someone else's eyes?

1022. What's the most recent decision you flipped on at the last second — and how did it turn out?

1023. How would you market the world's worst junk food as a "health" product — with a creative spin?

1024. What's one childhood nursery rhyme you can say word-for-word even now?

1025. Do you find yourself holding grudges longer than you should — and are you holding onto one right now?

1026. Do you have a locker room or changing room story that still makes you laugh or cringe today?

1027. What silly or helpful thing would you have a family member do if you could hypnotize them?

1028. What's the one pet name you really don't like hearing — even if it's meant affectionately?

1029. What's a time when someone talked you into something you didn't really want — and how did it turn out?

1030. What are the top three traits you look for in a true, trustworthy friend?

1031. Is there a canned fruit you think beats the fresh version in flavor or texture?

1032. Which guitar riff pumps you up the most whenever you hear it?

1033. How many disposable items do you use each week — and do you try to limit them?

1034. What's the cheesiest dad joke you secretly love telling?

1035. What celebrity chef's dishes would you politely avoid at all costs?

1036. What practical or playful skill do you think could be mastered with one month of focus?

1037. Where in the real world would you expect to find the magical lands of Middle Earth?

1038. How do you handle it when you know someone is full of hot air, but others believe them?

1039. What creative new name would you invent for guinea pigs since they're neither pigs nor from Guinea?

1040. After a tough day, what meal always feels like the ultimate comfort food to you?

1041. Can you remember the last time you walked barefoot outdoors — maybe on grass, sand, or a trail?

1042. Where did you eat the most expensive meal of your life — and would you do it again?

1043. Who do you know that's all about creativity, art, and maybe a little bit of quirky style?

1044. What situations or details set off your inner alarms and make you feel a little paranoid?

1045. How many slices of toast could you eat in a sitting if you were really hungry — and have you tried?

1046. Beard, mustache, goatee — what facial hair style do you like the most or think suits people well?

1047. How did your family handle it when you had chickenpox — any creative ways to keep you from scratching?

1048. Was there an animal you desperately wanted as a kid that you weren't allowed to have?

1049. If cash disappeared, what creative or meaningful things would you want to be paid with?

1050. What's the most recent thing you felt totally sure about, even if no one else agreed?

1051. Have you ever teased someone by calling them "Mr. or Ms. Fancy-Pants" — and what made you say it?

1052. What sound completely grossed you out when you heard it — even if it still makes you laugh now?

1053. Who's the one friend you wish you could "mute" every once in a while — just to get a little quiet?

1054. What martial art would you choose to instantly master — and what would you do with your new skill?

1055. What's a great people-watching moment you caught at the airport — funny, touching, or totally bizarre?

1056. You find a spider at home — do you capture it, crush it, or call for backup?

1057. What's one food you love but realize you've never seen how it looks before it's cooked or processed?

1058. How many clocks do you have in your house — and are you someone who keeps them all perfectly synchronized?

1059. What's a dream souvenir you'd love to pick up on an adventure abroad?

1060. What dog breed would you say reflects your attitude and style most closely?

1061. What funny or cool scent would you add to a soap bar — something bold or different?

1062. Have you ever spotted someone using something crazy to tie their hair back?

1063. Is there a conspiracy theory that you think could actually be possible?

1064. What age do you think strikes the best balance for having kids — energy, wisdom, stability?

1065. Would you describe yourself as artistic — and what creative skills are you proud of?

1066. How would you repurpose an empty ice cream tub into something fun or useful?

1067. If Prince William and Kate dropped by for tea, what would you proudly serve them?

1068. Which major global challenge do you think new tech will make huge progress solving soon?

1069. Do you maintain a journal — and if so, is it a daily habit or an occasional outlet for you?

1070. What's the most hilarious or unforgettable last name you've ever come across?

1071. Can you remember the last moment you felt those fluttery "butterflies" from excitement or nerves?

1072. Have you caught yourself doing something lately that reminded you of your father or mother?

1073. Should we assume someone is innocent until proven guilty — or should it be the other way around?

1074. What's the coolest or funniest hand shadow puppet you can create?

1075. What performer have you seen live who completely wowed you with outrageous energy or style?

1076. When you're firing up the grill, what's the one food you look forward to cooking the most?

1077. If you needed to make clothes from curtains, which room would you pick for the best fabric?

1078. What's the most recent dish you cooked without any shortcuts or premade ingredients?

1079. Would you take a $1,000 dare to attempt a ski jump — even if it was a little scary?

1080. What's the craziest or coolest basketball trick shot you've watched live or online?

1081. Who among your friends does the best villain-style evil laugh?

1082. What's the coolest or most ridiculous email address you've seen or used yourself?

1083. Have you ever embraced the moment and sang or danced during a rainstorm?

1084. If any land animal could suddenly swim underwater like a pro, which one would you choose?

1085. What would your WWE ring name be if you were stepping into the wrestling world?

1086. In a movie where you're an assassin, who would be your first fictional mission?

1087. Could you see robots taking over teaching — and would that be a good thing or a bad thing?

1088. What are the top three traits you look for when trusting someone as a friend?

1089. What's your reaction plan if you ever accidentally swallow a fly?

1090. What's the story behind the last time you walked out of a movie before it ended?

1091. Imagine you were aboard the Titanic — how would you have gotten onto a lifeboat?

1092. Is there a food from abroad you miss because it's hard or impossible to find where you are?

1093. What's the motto you live by that keeps you grounded and motivated?

1094. Where's the most isolated or empty-feeling place you've ever found yourself?

1095. Is it ever really fair to do anything in love or war, or are there lines you shouldn't cross?

1096. What's the most memorable (or messy) pancake toss you've ever attempted?

1097. What's the longest list of songs you can come up with that include numbers?

1098. What's the strangest tool you've ever grabbed when a pen wasn't around?

1099. What movie would be amazing if retold through the eyes of a side character?

1100. What's the coolest stunt or trick you've ever seen a trained animal perform?

1101. If you had to pick one body part to enlarge, which would it be — and why?

1102. If a vampire bit a zombie, what crazy outcome do you think would happen?

1103. When was the last time you flew a kite — and how did it go?

1104. Have you seen a really awesome or hilarious car sunshade — what did it look like?

1105. Have you ever felt love at first sight — or do you think it's just a sweet idea?

1106. What's the lowest percentage you usually allow your phone to reach before charging?

1107. What was a turning point in your life when you realized you couldn't undo the choice?

1108. What better ways could we measure real success beyond just money and recognition?

1109. What kind of time-saving invention would you create to make life easier?

1110. How do you usually react when another driver aggressively tailgates you?

1111. Would you risk a guaranteed $10,000 for a chance at $100,000 if you were 90% confident?

1112. If you had to pick the funniest name no royal would ever use for a baby, what would it be?

1113. You and your friends spot one slice of pizza left — how do you decide who gets it?

1114. What's a tiny annoyance that managed to irritate you more than it should have today?

1115. Did you ever get a Valentine's card from someone who never revealed who they were?

1116. What's a cool or funny name you would pick for a speedy racing greyhound?

1117. If you could erase one celebrity's influence from history, who would you choose?

1118. Which event from your life do you think will be remembered and taught about a century from now?

1119. When you think about your journey, who do you owe the biggest thank you to?

1120. What's one rule that, no matter the situation, you think should always be followed?

1121. How would you go about building new friendships if you found yourself in a new city?

1122. If the three little pigs lived in a crazy world, what wild things might they build their houses with?

1123. Who was the opponent the last time you found yourself in an epic snowball fight?

1124. What impressive bake would you bring to wow the judges on a baking competition?

1125. Have you inherited or kept a watch or jewelry item from a family member?

1126. Where's the oddest spot or surface you've ever fallen asleep on?

1127. Did you ever make a wish on a star — and did it happen for you?

1128. If you had to pick a theme song for your life, which one would you choose?

1129. If you could invent a new month, what would you name it — and what would it be like?

1130. If you had to trade three possessions to get the one thing you want most, what would you give up?

1131. Do you track your steps daily, and is hitting 10,000 part of your goal?

1132. If you could pick a hilariously complicated team name just to challenge the cheerleaders, what would it be?

1133. Who would you love to shadow for a day to understand how they navigate life and challenges?

1134. When was the last time you entered a competition or felt a strong competitive spirit?

1135. If you could eat anywhere tonight without worrying about cost, where would you go?

1136. What tends to stir up strong memories or feelings of nostalgia for you?

1137. What's a funny or surprising word that has a very different meaning in another country?

1138. Have you ever heard a great response to someone making a short/tall joke? What was it?

1139. Who among your friends is definitely the "loud and proud" type — and do you admire it?

1140. If you had to pick a bold or memorable pen name as an author, what would it be?

1141. What's the biggest threat you believe could someday cause humanity's downfall?

1142. What historical or famous figure would you want to bring to life in a movie?

1143. What's your best (or most hilarious) experience ever from being in a hot tub?

1144. If NYC cabs had to change color, what new look would you give them?

1145. What's a word that feels great rolling off the tongue — fun, strong, or silly?

1146. Have you ever missed remembering a close family member's birthday? What happened?

1147. What bold or hilarious name would you give a company that goes head-to-head with Amazon?

1148. Does growing up without siblings mean you miss important parts of life — or just live it differently?

1149. What fun word would you invent to describe a habit you just can't seem to break?

1150. What video game world would you love to live in for 24 hours — adventure, action, or fun?

1151. What old-school game from your childhood would today's kids find strange or fun?

1152. When did you wish you could be in two different places at the same time?

1153. How do you cope when you're lying awake and sleep just won't come?

1154. Which company, factory, or secret place would you love to explore on a private tour?

1155. Are you a fan of dunking biscuits in tea like Queen Victoria — or do you avoid the soggy drama?

1156. What was your last hands-on DIY project — fixing something, building, or creating?

1157. What did you do to mark your last birthday — and was it memorable?

1158. Which landmark lit up at night left a lasting impression on you?

1159. Can you remember the last time you had a nosebleed — and where you were when it happened?

1160. What should the "official" consequence be if someone sneaks food off your plate?

1161. Without water available, what's your drink of choice to beat thirst?

1162. What achievement, big or small, made you brag a little recently?

1163. What new Lego set idea would you invent to bring fun and creativity to life?

1164. What's a superpower you think would be more of a curse than a gift?

1165. Where do you imagine the mysterious lost city of Atlantis could be discovered someday?

1166. How would you design your own paradise — the sights, sounds, and experiences?

1167. What powerful or funny tagline would you invent to rival "Just do it" for a sports brand?

1168. If you were filling a time capsule today, what five things would you include to represent life right now?

1169. How would your routines change if you had to pedal to generate electricity for your home?

1170. What would be your strategy if you had to escape a charging elephant?

1171. Can you remember a time when you were the very last to hear some important news?

1172. What's the noisiest event or sound you've ever experienced firsthand?

1173. Would you be excited or reluctant to serve on a jury for a high-profile trial?

1174. What was the last cool find you picked up — or meaningful thing you donated — to a thrift shop?

1175. Which friend seems to come up with endless ideas — whether brilliant, wild, or both?

1176. When mid-afternoon hunger hits, what's your snack of choice?

1177. What essentials do you carry in your pockets most days?

1178. What futuristic upgrade do you think cars will include as standard someday?

1179. What issue or cause would motivate you to step up and march in protest?

1180. What inspires a strong sense of pride and patriotism in you?

1181. Have you ever knocked your funny bone and found yourself laughing instead of complaining?

1182. What stick-food do you think is absolutely the best — tasty and fun?

1183. Would you be willing to thumb a ride if your car broke down and you had no other option?

1184. What's your record for the longest (and maybe most frustrating) hold time on the phone?

1185. Which electronics do you leave running or charging 24/7 at home?

1186. Would you discreetly point it out if someone had toilet paper trailing from their shoe?

1187. Would you support adding jousting to the modern Olympic Games for fun and tradition?

1188. Have you ever had a home remedy attempt totally backfire? What happened?

1189. Is there a signature dish or drink your hometown is proud of?

1190. Can you think of something important that was lost in history and will probably stay lost?

1191. Who do you hope will be there cheering you on when you turn 90?

1192. Which sports hero, celebrity, or legend would you love to have a signed picture from?

1193. What fierce or funny name would you add to the official list of hurricane names?

1194. What alternate name would you create for Smurfs if you had the chance?

1195. Have you ever totally misheard a song lyric? What did you think it said?

1196. What did you put out for Santa Claus and his reindeer when you were a kid?

1197. Have you heard a hilarious story of identical twins switching places as a prank?

1198. Which swimming stroke would you master if you were an Olympic athlete?

1199. What would be your top three improvements if you could redesign your work life?

1200. What's the story behind the last time you gave flowers to someone?

1201. In a wacky world, what would Yankee Doodle stick in his cap instead of a feather?

1202. Have you ever had a dream so vivid that you acted on it, thinking it really happened?

1203. What fun or bold phrase would you add to candy hearts for Valentine's Day?

1204. What would be your survival plan if you were trapped by an avalanche?

1205. Which of the seven dwarfs do you think matches your personality the best?

1206. What's a personalized license plate you saw that made you laugh or think?

1207. Do you know anyone who loves throwing out tech terms even when it's not needed?

1208. What unforgettable experience would you choose to relive as if it were brand new?

1209. What's a piece of information someone shared with you that you wish they had kept to themselves?

1210. What's your go-to trick if you blank on someone's name during introductions?

1211. What's the weirdest profession you've ever come across in real life?

1212. Have you ever deleted something valuable by mistake? What was it?

1213. If you could have the foot of any animal instead of your own, what would you choose?

1214. Which once-in-a-lifetime moment would you jump at the chance to relive?

1215. Who would you officially crown as the King of Pop — past or present?

1216. What cool or funny emoji would you design to fill a gap in how we express ourselves?

1217. If life came with guarantees, what's one thing you would want locked in for sure?

1218. If Hogwarts existed in another universe, what strange or awesome subject would it specialize in?

1219. What's your take: is fate real, or do we make our own paths?

1220. What's your best strategy for escaping a long-winded talker?

1221. If you could make a part of your body give off a warning sound, what would it be — and what sound?

1222. Tell me about your worst haircut experience. How bad was it?

1223. If you could mash up two crazy skills, like breakdancing and magic, what would they be?

1224. What's the film you've rewatched the most, and why does it stick with you?

1225. Has a TV commercial ever caught you off guard and made you emotional?

1226. When's the last time you were sweating buckets — and what were you doing?

1227. If music didn't exist, what part of your daily life would feel emptiest?

1228. What motivating or funny message would you hide inside a chocolate treat?

1229. What normal household item would make the coolest hidden James Bond gadget?

1230. Which gesture or hand sign is understood pretty much everywhere?

1231. Could you bring yourself to stroke a cockroach if you had to?

1232. What recent appointment or outing did you have to cancel at the last minute?

1233. In your home, is there a seat that's considered "off-limits" because it's someone's favorite?

1234. Has anything resurfaced lately — a memory or feeling — that you'd rather not think about?

1235. Which famous figure would you actually enjoy being trapped in an elevator with for a few hours?

1236. Which impressive or massive bridge have you traveled across — and where?

1237. Should there be a rule that people above a certain income must help charities? What's your take?

1238. When was a time you went a long stretch without talking to a close friend or family member?

1239. How many steps would you get running from danger before you needed a breather?

1240. Which world record would you want to hold — whether impressive, weird, or hilarious?

1241. Is happiness, in your view, a decision or something that depends on circumstances?

1242. What's the story behind the last homemade gift you gave or received?

1243. What funny or creative new name could you give The Lion, the Witch and the Wardrobe?

1244. What important keys do you still carry, and which one would cause you the most trouble if lost?

1245. What bizarre item have you spotted strapped to the top of a vehicle?

1246. How many kids in a family do you think is just a little too much to handle?

1247. What new jelly bean flavor would you love to create?

1248. What music would you want to play each time you sneezed, just for fun?

1249. What sight, big or small, always brings a smile to your face?

1250. Is outdoor live music better than indoor concerts, or do you prefer the energy inside?

1251. How do you shake off sleep and kickstart your mornings?

1252. Would you be comfortable catching a movie solo? Have you ever done it?

1253. If someone offered you one priceless jewelry item, what would you choose?

1254. Who would you most enjoy having a no-holds-barred water pistol showdown with?

1255. Which file on your computer do you protect the most because it's that important?

1256. What's the most memorable way curiosity landed you in hot water?

1257. What's a Google Doodle you thought was especially cool, fun, or moving?

1258. If you ended up getting arrested, even unfairly, what would people assume you did?

1259. What funny or heartfelt greeting card verse would you love to write?

1260. What retro slang word should people start using again because it's just too good?

1261. What meaningful wish would you make come true for someone you care about?

1262. What purchases do you absolutely always research online first?

1263. What was your first-ever cellphone — and how do you remember feeling about it?

1264. Would you spend six months at the International Space Station if given the chance?

1265. When's the last time you defended someone who needed support?

1266. What bold or strong new name would fit Nike if it ever needed a rebrand?

1267. What's your best (or most embarrassing) gym story?

1268. Have you ever stumbled onto information you weren't supposed to find out?

1269. What's your main go-to device for snapping pictures these days?

1270. Who would feel your absence the most if you suddenly vanished?

1271. What's your go-to movie for guaranteed laughter, even if you've seen it a hundred times?

1272. How would you quickly spend $1,000 if you had just sixty minutes to use it?

1273. What cut or style of jeans do you wear the most — and why does it suit you?

1274. Where would it be the worst — and most hilarious — place to accidentally break wind?

1275. What action would you make illegal for just one day to make life better?

1276. What's the last activity that gave you an unforgettable adrenaline rush?

1277. What crazy new escape stunt would Harry Houdini have dreamed up if he'd survived?

1278. What's something you've seen time and again that almost never ends well?

1279. Have you ever gotten a funny nickname just because someone mispronounced your name?

1280. What hashtag did you last invent — either seriously or as a joke?

1281. What cool or funny names would you pick for three penguins at a zoo?

1282. What's your go-to victory phrase when you win at something?

1283. What age do you believe is the right time for someone to hang up their work boots?

1284. Is there a hearty or seasonal food you only crave in the colder months?

1285. What unique or nostalgic smell would make an awesome candle scent?

1286. How many shoe sizes would you have grown today if food thoughts made your feet bigger?

1287. When was the last time you were absolutely stunned into silence?

1288. What feature stands out to you most when you notice someone attractive?

1289. Have you ever proudly won an argument only to find out later you were wrong?

1290. If you could set a punishment for middle-lane hoggers, what would it be?

1291. Who's the funniest person you know who can wiggle their ears — or other odd talents?

1292. What's something safe but gross you absolutely won't touch with your bare hands?

1293. Have you ever found something valuable or hilarious hidden in an old jacket?

1294. What's something you suggested to someone recently because you loved it?

1295. If you had to pick a Mr. Men or Little Miss character to represent you, who would it be?

1296. If your weekly meal plan was locked in, what would you love to eat every Wednesday?

1297. If you could redesign chess pieces with a crazy or funny theme, what would you pick?

1298. Would you dare to walk across hot coals if it meant proving something to yourself?

1299. What would be a fun or important subject to create an entire encyclopedia about today?

1300. What's your best or funniest reason for ever getting detention?

1301. What track would you choose to help you stay in rhythm during CPR chest compressions?

1302. What's your opinion on banning loot boxes in games aimed at younger players?

1303. Have you ever had a great or hilarious experience while dining at a fancy place?

1304. What's one food you absolutely draw the line at and would never eat?

1305. What's the most unbelievable nanny cam story you've heard?

1306. If the Six Million Dollar Man were rebuilt today, what astronomical price tag would he carry?

1307. What goes through your mind when you see just one shoe lying alone on the road?

1308. Would you trust a ghostwriter to tell your life story, or would you insist on writing it yourself?

1309. If you spotted a woman crying on a park bench, would you approach her or keep walking?

1310. What would you do if you caught someone stealing a simple item at a store?

1311. Have you ever been someone's hero, even if you didn't realize it at the time?

1312. What's your move when loud chatter ruins your movie theater experience?

1313. What food would deserve a whole poem if you were to write one today?

1314. When was the last time you touched something way hotter than you expected?

1315. What's your favorite-scented spray product you use?

1316. What do you predict will be the next thing people ban or outlaw?

1317. What bold or creative look would you give to new paper bills if you could redesign them?

1318. Which Jungle Book character would you want to adventure with for a day?

1319. Which celebrity or character would make the perfect GPS voice for your trips?

1320. What was your worst school subject — and did you ever fail it?

1321. What's your average yearly book count — and are you proud of it?

1322. What hilarious mask would make a modern-day bank robbery scene unforgettable?

1323. What wild or awesome ice cream flavor would you create if you could?

1324. What's an experience or thing that's always better the first time and less exciting later?

1325. What's a moment where you were totally confused, and how did you handle it?

1326. What's your ideal way to have a steak cooked — and what details matter most?

1327. What playful new names would you invent for boy and girl goats?

1328. What's a line that would totally ruin the mood if someone said it at a wedding?

1329. What other foods or drinks should come in quick "bags" like tea or coffee?

1330. What's a positive news story you recently came across and loved?

1331. What's one simple feature you'd add to improve the human body?

1332. What's the weirdest object you've seen turned into an instrument?

1333. What old-fashioned holiday would you redesign for today's world?

1334. What daring adventure would you take on if you knew falling wasn't possible?

1335. What stylish or fun name would you give a new men's spa or grooming place?

1336. Have you ever had a haircut, style, or grooming disaster you still laugh about?

1337. Who's your dream or real-life crew for re-enacting the "Bohemian Rhapsody" headbang?

1338. What's the weirdest or best natural fix for constipation you know of?

1339. Do you believe someone's nature can change over time, or do they stay the same?

1340. What's a recent moment where you thought, "I can't believe I did that"?

1341. How would your lifestyle and work change if cell phones didn't exist?

1342. What's a cool or mind-blowing dinosaur fact you love sharing?

1343. What's your worst sunburn story — and did you learn your lesson?

1344. What's your reaction when someone invades your personal bubble?

1345. Which buddy would you pick to swap fingers with, just for fun?

1346. What's the coolest illusion or magic stunt you've ever seen live or on video?

1347. Are you the guy your friends would rely on in a real emergency?

1348. Could you manage your everyday activities if you were limited to one arm?

1349. What's a smart or surprising tip for staying youthful that you've actually used?

1350. What's a family tradition that's been honored through generations in your family?

1351. What's the coolest or most useful thing you've ever seen made from recycling?

1352. Have you ever forced yourself into a cold shower? What was it like?

1353. What's your personal signal that winter is ending and spring is starting?

1354. If you had a leap year birthday, what day would you pick for your party in normal years?

1355. Which athletes, if any, do you think are paid way more than they should be?

1356. What's your proudest high score on a test or exam?

1357. If you planted magic beans, what wild and powerful thing would sprout?

1358. What's the longest time you've ever stayed inside without stepping outdoors?

1359. What one powerful or meaningful word would you want to add to life's storybook?

1360. When approached by someone asking for money on the street, what do you usually do?

1361. What funny name would you give to the sound of a yawn and a burp happening together?

1362. What's your longest sleepless streak, and what made you pull it off?

1363. How many official names of bones could you list without checking?

1364. What's the everyday sight that reminds you of how beautiful life can be?

1365. When's the last moment you felt the wind whip past you and it made you feel alive?

1366. What's the craziest color you've ever worn on your pants — and why?

1367. What's the ultimate towel origami design you would love to master?

1368. What's the most mind-blowing thing you've learned from a documentary?

1369. What place or activity sparks your best ideas when you're stuck?

1370. What's the most romantic thing someone has done that really impressed you?

1371. What awesome or adventurous theme would you create for a hotel room?

1372. When something great happens, who's the first person you call or text?

1373. What's one thing you do well that you know you can count on?

1374. What's something that deserved a "zero rating" from you, and why?

1375. What pizza topping do you think never should have made it to a menu?

1376. Who was your least favorite teacher growing up, and what made them tough for you?

1377. What's the most daring or gutsy thing you've ever tried?

1378. How mindful are you about chewing your food before you swallow?

1379. What's the nastiest food combo you've witnessed a friend eat and enjoy?

1380. What games or tunes kept you entertained on long family road trips?

1381. What's a "great idea" you had that ended up being not so great after all?

1382. What task or activity do you think is super easy while others struggle with it?

1383. What's your best memory or crazy moment from being inside a bounce house?

1384. What's your take on UFOs — and have you ever witnessed one yourself?

1385. What's the longest traffic jam you've survived, and what was the trip for?

1386. If you couldn't call it a ponytail, what wild animal feature would describe your hairstyle?

1387. What three words would you use to sum up the experience of real love?

1388. When have you found yourself in the spotlight unexpectedly and didn't enjoy it?

1389. What's the most adorable or heart-melting thing you've ever seen?

1390. Do you think there's a reason behind everything that happens in life?

1391. What twist would you add to marathon races to make them way more entertaining?

1392. As a world-famous cat burglar, what bold item would you steal for your "career highlight"?

1393. What habit or behavior did you catch yourself doing — even though it bothers you when others do it?

1394. How many times do you think you glance at your phone daily?

1395. What's the most battery-hungry gadget or device you own?

1396. What's the best meal you could whip up right now with just what's sitting in your fridge?

1397. If you could invent a clever clothing hybrid like "skorts," what would it be called?

1398. What everyday experiences convince you that life isn't just a computer program?

1399. How do you think positive or negative thoughts can impact real life?

1400. What's one health trend or rule you refuse to follow?

1401. When has your gut instinct warned you about something and been correct?

1402. What do you find most distracting when you're trying to concentrate on something important?

1403. Is there somewhere you're not welcome anymore — and what's the story behind it?

1404. What funny or clever phrase would you train a parrot to say?

1405. Do you think there's always a bright side to difficult times?

1406. What's the silliest object you've ever managed to poke yourself in the eye with?

1407. When was the last time you kicked off your shoes and felt sand between your toes?

1408. What new shape would you design, and what bold name would you give it?

1409. Who's the loudest nose-blower among your friends or family?

1410. What wild fundraising challenge would you invent to go viral for charity?

1411. What would make today even better and put you in an amazing mood?

1412. What sweet treat from your family traditions would belong in a recipe collection?

1413. What's the boldest way you've ever avoided people when you needed alone time?

1414. Should marriages be treated like annual contracts you agree to renew — or not?

1415. If you had to pick one Thomas character that matches your personality, who would it be?

1416. Whose tattoos have impressed you the most, and what makes them stand out?

1417. What's the greatest life story or lesson an elder has shared with you?

1418. Are you someone who wears socks to bed — and do you feel it's a good or bad idea?

1419. What hilarious or ridiculous hedge shape would you create in a garden?

1420. Would you choose to be the "wheelbarrow" or the runner in a field day race?

1421. What's the weirdest thing a fan asked a celebrity to autograph?

1422. What three features would you add to your own original family board game?

1423. What subject sucked you into a long Wikipedia binge last time?

1424. Where and when did you have your very first kiss?

1425. What's the hardest habit you have that you think you couldn't easily change?

1426. Which school sports did you enjoy the most growing up?

1427. How many times today have you caught yourself checking the mirror?

1428. Which hot meal would be hardest for you to give up if you had to eat only cold food?

1429. Where were you when you reached the highest altitude you've ever been?

1430. Is there a certain order you always follow when putting on your clothes?

1431. What's a question you believe will always stay a mystery?

1432. What food name always makes you laugh because it doesn't match the ingredients?

1433. Are you more of a Coke guy or a Pepsi guy — and what makes you say that?

1434. What's your wildest or funniest babysitting memory?

1435. What's the weirdest thing you remember stuffing in your nose or ear as a kid?

1436. What valuable thing do you have that money could never replace?

1437. What TV channel would you choose if you had to live with only one?

1438. What plain-colored animal do you think would look cooler with stripes?

1439. Did you ever try a celebrity-inspired haircut? How did it turn out?

1440. Which film would you love to see a follow-up made for?

1441. What's the best or funniest victory dance you've seen someone pull off?

1442. What childhood playground games are now banned or discouraged?

1443. What's the best prize you've ever walked away with?

1444. Which one of the "seven deadly sins" would you say tempts you the most?

1445. What's the most convincing way you could argue that the world is flat (even if you don't believe it)?

1446. If you had to describe your style in three words, what would they be?

1447. Where would you want your ashes scattered if you could pick any special spot?

1448. What's the wisest or most powerful advice you've ever been given?

1449. What's the most hilarious outfit you own that would be terrible for outdoor sports?

1450. Who was the guy everyone knew at your school, and what made him so liked?

1451. What's the most spectacular food or drink disaster you've caused by dropping it?

1452. If you kept failing your driving test, how many tries would it take before you'd call it quits?

1453. Which famous person would make the worst ballroom dancing partner for you?

1454. What explanation do you usually come up with for bumps in the night?

1455. What creative symbol would you use instead of "the fat lady sings" to mark the end?

1456. What's the last decision you made that you regretted immediately?

1457. Which influencer do you actually look up to, and what do you admire about them?

1458. What's your go-to, unbeatable toast topping?

1459. Your shoes are gone after swimming — how would you handle it?

1460. What's the most outrageous thing you've seen added to a hot dog?

1461. What's something you've wound by hand — a toy, clock, or something else?

1462. What's the most rare or special thing you think exists in the world?

1463. What was the most recent thing that made you feel totally out of your element?

1464. What's the worst thing you can imagine discovering stuffed inside an old coat?

1465. How many things have you started but not finished at the moment?

1466. How would Snow White and the Seven Dwarfs change if you flipped the whole story?

1467. What's a time you looked guilty even though you hadn't done anything?

1468. Where are the most northern and southern places you've been?

1469. What's something you think people should be allowed to do at a younger age?

1470. Is there anything you have that you wish was a different color?

1471. What bold new slogan would you create for Greta Thunberg's mission?

1472. What big land animal would be the most impressive flying through the sky?

1473. What outside experience would you miss the most if you could never leave home?

1474. Which musical instrument has the saddest, most soulful sound to your ears?

1475. What's your funniest story about trying (and failing) to be super quiet?

1476. Could you sing your national anthem from start to finish without looking up the words?

1477. How would you cleverly get the attention of noisy kids without yelling?

1478. Would you use your parents' discipline methods, or would you do it differently?

1479. What's the last clumsy or awkward moment you really hoped stayed private?

1480. What's a modern twist on what Jack and Jill could go get?

1481. What part of your face do you most appreciate just the way it is?

1482. What part of your routine would be hardest to give up without internet?

1483. What's the worst thing you could order to eat on a first date?

1484. What's the last win or success that made you feel unstoppable?

1485. What crazy substitute would you suggest for the horses in the Pony Express?

1486. What TV show would be the hardest to give up forever?

1487. What new character would make Clue even more interesting?

1488. What magazine subscription have you had that you really looked forward to?

1489. What album do you listen to all the way through without skipping any tracks?

1490. What's the slang word you say the most without even realizing it?

1491. Can you usually guess a song right away just by the intro?

1492. What's the clearest example you've experienced that proved nothing in life is truly free?

1493. What animals would make the most hilarious mismatched racing opponents?

1494. What's something valuable you want that can't be bought with cash?

1495. How would you spend a million dollars to truly make a difference?

1496. What's your must-have chocolate from the box when you get first choice?

1497. Walking backward for a whole day — what activity would be the most ridiculous?

1498. If Ed Sheeran had to write a song about something ridiculous, what should it be?

1499. When you were young, what age seemed like it was "basically ancient"?

1500. What's the story of an animal you've rescued?

1501. What part of the day feels most like "your time"?

1502. If you needed to clear space fast, what three things would you toss?

1503. What tune has been stubbornly stuck in your mind recently?

1504. Does knowing others have bigger challenges help you stay grateful?

1505. Which famous quote could totally work as a slogan for sneakers or shoes?

1506. Have you ever sat confused while everyone else cracked up? What was the joke?

1507. What's the last small luxury or indulgence you treated yourself to?

1508. How often do you fire up the kettle in a regular day?

1509. What non-violent but irritating thing would make someone crack fast?

1510. What song changed for you once you actually listened to the words?

1511. What well-known figure would you want guiding your journey?

1512. Who's the person you've struggled to forgive the longest?

1513. How old is too old to bust a move like you're in a street dance battle?

1514. Which classic childhood game should definitely become an Olympic competition?

1515. What's the craziest story a grandparent told you that you still wonder about?

1516. What kind of "on hold" music drives you absolutely nuts?

1517. Are mass balloon releases a tradition that needs to end for good?

1518. What was the last GIF you used to react to something funny or crazy?

1519. What funny name would you give to a brand new, crazy type of cheese?

1520. What's one thing you've gained or achieved since this time last year?

1521. When did you first try using chopsticks — and how did it go?

1522. What popular myth would you love to bust and reveal the truth about?

1523. Who do you know that got a small amount of authority and went a little overboard?

1524. What's the coolest or weirdest thing you've ever rescued from the trash?

1525. Imagine you're penning a hit song — what would you rhyme with "jet-black hair"?

1526. What penalty would you give to people who toss garbage where it doesn't belong?

1527. What favorite chewy meal would you mourn if you could only eat soft foods?

1528. Which buddy would you nominate for worst table manners at a dinner?

1529. What names were all over the playground the year you were born?

1530. Imagine the chaos if every toilet on Earth flushed together — what would happen?

1531. What store would you love a $500 gift card for right now?

1532. Who was your last movie buddy at the cinema and what was the film?

1533. Which current piece of tech do you think is heading for extinction first?

1534. What's the weirdest or wildest plant you've ever heard of?

1535. What cool bonus feature would you build into a watch?

1536. Trapped in an elevator for hours — what food would you want delivered to survive?

1537. What three traits do you think make a guy someone others want to be around?

1538. You've got $50 to brighten someone's day — what would you do?

1539. When the zombies come, what survival skill would you bring to the group?

1540. When you did the mannequin challenge, what was your "freeze frame" pose?

1541. What's the wildest discovery you can imagine happening on Mars?

1542. Can you remember a time you made an impact that mattered?

1543. What's a non-weapon object that would raise eyebrows on a flight?

1544. If someone knocked during a storm, would you answer or stay put?

1545. When you were a kid, what did you name your two favorite toys?

1546. What's the last app, file, or song you downloaded?

1547. For one day, if you had an animal's teeth, which would you choose and why?

1548. What's one thing you've done to make a positive impact in the world?

1549. When was the last time you were so happy you cried?

1550. Do you think robots could ever take over, and does it worry you?

1551. What's the best deal you've ever scored at a dollar store?

1552. Ever gone to work or school wearing yesterday's boxers/briefs?

1553. Which job do you think doesn't get enough credit for how hard it is?

1554. How much money would it take for you to feel completely secure?

1555. What's the craziest move you've pulled while running on no sleep?

1556. No matter how it's hidden, what taste always stands out to you?

1557. What gluten-free vegan meal would you throw together if you had to?

1558. What fierce or funny name would you give a plant that could eat people?

1559. What's a tiny victory that always makes you feel like a champ?

1560. What's a good manly alternative to saying "as old as the hills"?

1561. What advice would you pass down to your ten-year-old version of yourself?

1562. Has anyone compared you to a famous man? Who was it?

1563. What's the grossest thing you've ever come across inside a jar?

1564. What's the last thing someone did that almost made you yell in frustration?

1565. What food smell would you outlaw in confined spaces like buses or trains?

1566. Is there really no such thing as a dumb question, or are some exceptions?

1567. What's something you're obsessed with more than cats are with boxes?

1568. Have you ever tested the myth of frying an egg on a hot car?

1569. What's the most brilliant but lazy shortcut you've seen someone pull off?

1570. What cloud number would you pick instead of nine, and why?

1571. What crazy or funny medals would exist at the Olympics in an alternate world?

1572. Who was the last person you checked in on at the hospital?

1573. What's the most jaw-dropping natural sight you've ever laid eyes on?

1574. What's a music genre you just can't stand listening to?

1575. What's the one quality that makes a relationship last?

1576. Which buddy of yours is a grump sometimes, and what do you do about it?

1577. What would you do if rare animals were destroying rare plants?

1578. If you're rhyming with "looking at the sun," what fun line would you write?

1579. What's your wildest "bad neighbor" experience?

1580. If limited to one clothing item a year, what would you pick?

1581. What bold new chip flavor would you love to create?

1582. How many musical groups with numbers in their names can you list?

1583. What hilarious item would you bury to puzzle archaeologists someday?

1584. What's your best memory from a drive-in movie theater?

1585. What's one challenge you thought would be easy but wasn't?

1586. What jackpot amount would convince you to leave your job?

1587. What famous speech or poem would you like to deliver from memory?

1588. What's the most memorable place you've seen fireworks?

1589. What's something awesome you found on TV without planning?

1590. Which relative of yours is a real tea expert?

1591. What's the strangest vehicle or ride you've ever used?

1592. Would you have signed up or refused to fight if drafted in WWI?

1593. What desperate tactics have you seen tired new dads or moms use?

1594. What's the harshest nickname you've ever given someone?

1595. What's the softest thing you've touched — like velvet or fur?

1596. What was the last favor a friend asked you to do?

1597. What guilty pleasure food would you be embarrassed to admit liking?

1598. If Usain Bolt chased you, how long a head start would you need to beat him to the kitchen?

1599. What's the worst "fashion over comfort" choice you've made?

1600. What university degree seems least useful for real-world work?

1601. What's the most unbelievable but real reason someone gave for missing an event?

1602. What other shape would bananas be if they weren't curved?

1603. How late were you allowed to stay up when you were ten?

1604. During a power outage on a Saturday night, what would you do to pass the time?

1605. What's the worst haircut you ever rocked in an old photo?

1606. How do you handle removing a stuck bandage without wincing?

1607. What's something you thought would be awful but wasn't so bad after all?

1608. Did the movie Jaws ever make you hesitate before going swimming?

1609. What's the coolest part about being the person you are?

1610. Where would you focus during a one-minute weekly shower?

1611. Which of your buddies has the cheesiest-smelling socks?

1612. What hilarious word did you use as a child when you couldn't say the real one?

1613. What's the dirtiest trick or worst thing you've ever pulled?

1614. Has crime ever been worth it in any story or example you know? Why?

1615. What's the most mind-blowing drone shot you've seen?

1616. What's the weirdest prized item someone has shown off to you?

1617. What bold new color would you pick for toilet paper to make bathrooms funnier?

1618. When did good luck last seem to be truly on your side?

1619. What's the most impressive balloon sculpture you've watched someone make?

1620. What activity would be impossible if you had to wear clown shoes?

1621. What rugged or genius gadget would you add to a Swiss army knife?

1622. What hearty meal could you whip up if lentils were the main ingredient?

1623. What's the funniest knock-knock joke you've got?

1624. What competitive events would you add to a "guys' Olympics" at work?

1625. What's the most powerful quote about strength or resilience that sticks with you?

1626. Do you think mandatory organ donation shows strength of character?

1627. What's the farthest ahead you've ever bought sports or concert tickets?

1628. Which cartoon you grew up with was "wrecked" by a new version?

1629. Has anyone ever started a ridiculous rumor about you that made you laugh?

1630. What fierce or cool name would you give your pet dragon?

1631. What's one strength you'd focus on to become the man you want to be?

1632. If you gave up flying, how much would it change your work or adventure plans?

1633. If you could create a "Hall of Toughness," who would you put in first?

1634. In your experience, what qualities or things do women seem to treasure most?

1635. What is a memorable roast or jab you have delivered or heard in a playful setting?

1636. What strange item would make a wall of fame people couldnâ€™t resist visiting?

1637. Has ignoring a warning ever come back to bite you?

1638. Can you recall a moment you held back from reacting, even when you were seriously provoked?

1639. Which kind of cap or headgear would match your daily hustle if it had to be part of your wardrobe?

1640. When was the last time you built something just for the challenge—what was it?

1641. If you wrote a thriller where insects rise up, what would the title and main twist be?

1642. Which buddy has a sneeze so loud or strange that it's practically a party trick?

1643. What's your favorite band that's named after a color—and why do you like them?

1644. Imagine you're designing a quirky action figure for an animated adventure—what would it look like?

1645. If your voice suddenly had a new accent, which one would make you sound cooler?

1646. What idea did you once push against but now see as just part of the process?

1647. Could you take the cockpit under pressure if a voice guided you through the landing step-by-step?

1648. What's the funniest or cleverest tribute band name you've ever heard—or could make up?

1649. What small recognition in school made you feel like a champion, even if it wasn't flashy?

1650. What snack would you secretly celebrate being banned for health reasons?

1651. What single color would dominate your casual closet if you had to wear it daily?

1652. When was the last time something minor pushed your buttons enough to go on a full-blown rant?

1653. What's the most hands-on experience you've had growing something from the ground up?

1654. Is there a landmark or spot nearby that tourists love but you barely notice anymore?

1655. How did you deal with breakouts growing up—and what worked (or didn't)?

1656. What jelly bean color do you secretly hoard in the bag before anyone else gets to it?

1657. What would money look like if it were made from something rugged—like denim or metal?

1658. Have you ever built a collection of gear, cards, or tools—what was your favorite item?

1659. What's your go-to salty snack or favorite dish to season just right?

1660. Who do you still call using a home or office landline—and why?

1661. What's the weirdest or most delicious combo you've tried with ketchup?

1662. Who's the ultimate partner you'd want beside you as the credits roll on your life's story?

1663. If you were plotting a mystery, where would your antagonist stash the evidence?

1664. Is there a landmark or spot nearby that tourists love but you barely notice anymore?

1665. How did you deal with breakouts growing up—and what worked (or didn't)?

1666. What jelly bean color do you secretly hoard in the bag before anyone else gets to it?

1667. What would money look like if it were made from something rugged—like denim or metal?

1668. Have you ever built a collection of gear, cards, or tools—what was your favorite item?

1669. What's your go-to salty snack or favorite dish to season just right?

1670. Who do you still call using a home or office landline—and why?

1671. What's the weirdest or most delicious combo you've tried with ketchup?

1672. Who's the ultimate partner you'd want beside you as the credits roll on your life's story?

1673. If you were plotting a mystery, where would your antagonist stash the evidence?

1674. What small, reliable pick-me-up gets you through a tough afternoon?

1675. What product would make you walk away from a sales job on day one?

1676. What's one totally wrong thing you believed as a kid?

1677. Can you name a product you were surprised to learn has a different name abroad?

1678. Who pulled off a surprise that completely blew you away?

1679. What chip flavor would make the perfect lifelong snack companion?

1680. Have you seen a T-shirt with a phrase so bold you almost bought it?

1681. Did you or your friends ever go through a phase where all you listened to was emo or punk rock?

1682. If you had to pick a nursery rhyme figure to represent you, who would it be?

1683. How would your day look if you could skip traffic and arrive instantly?

1684. Was there a trend you envied as a teen but weren't allowed to try—like long hair, band tees, or sneakers?

1685. What's a funny or practical name you'd give to pants that everyone around the world could use?

1686. What's your best hack for managing headphone wires while on the move?

1687. What's the most "you" statement or joke you'd put on a T-shirt?

1688. No matter your schedule, who is the one guy you'll always show up for?

1689. What real-life stuff would you write about in a "man-to-man" advice column?

1690. Whether it's bratwurst or spicy chorizo, what sausage gets your vote at a BBQ?

1691. Who did you last send a pic to—was it a funny meme, a project, or something random?

1692. What's the funniest prank, joke, or comeback you pulled off in class?

1693. In a moment of crisis, what item would you save that means the most to you?

1694. What's the most masculine or meaningful item you've owned with your name on it?

1695. What was your first boys' sleepover like—who was there and what did you do?

1696. What's the most crowded event you've attended—sports, concert, rally?

1697. Are you the kind of guy who likes to rearrange furniture or keep it simple?

1698. What's the most chaotic or hilarious moment you've had while hosting or attending a dinner?

1699. Which guy in your circle tends to make a scene over the smallest thing?

1700. Is there a guy-food that's hyped but too messy or complicated to be worth it?

1701. What guy-worthy name would you give to a double sneeze + toot moment?

1702. What's your next big guy-purchase you're working toward—gear, tools, travel?

1703. What's the ultimate roast dinner lineup from your perspective—meat, sides, sauces?

1704. Have you ever challenged a rule and felt justified doing so?

1705. What's the guy code punishment for that fridge offense?

1706. Can you name four-piece rock or rap groups you've followed over the years?

1707. What tool did you grab last to fix something at home or work?

1708. What's the story behind your last black eye, if you've had one?

1709. Are you more of a Jerry, George, Kramer, or Newman—and how so?

1710. What's your go-to technique for tackling a tough pineapple like a pro?

1711. What bold or funny name would you give your dream fishing or speed boat?

1712. Would you be straight-up with a friend, even if it stings?

1713. When you lift your glass, what's your signature toast for the guys?

1714. Have you ever challenged a rule and felt justified doing so?

1715. What's the guy code punishment for that fridge offense?

1716. Can you name four-piece rock or rap groups you've followed over the years?

1717. What tool did you grab last to fix something at home or work?

1718. What's the story behind your last black eye, if you've had one?

1719. Are you more of a Jerry, George, Kramer, or Newman—and how so?

1720. What's your go-to technique for tackling a tough pineapple like a pro?

1721. What bold or funny name would you give your dream fishing or speed boat?

1722. Would you be straight-up with a friend, even if it stings?

1723. When you lift your glass, what's your signature toast for the guys?

1724. What's the most bizarre or unexpected questionnaire you've ever completed?

1725. What is the most practical or interesting course you've ever finished?

1726. What is your ultimate recipe for hot chocolate that hits the spot every time?

1727. If money and time were no issue, which five places are on your must-visit list?

1728. Which instrument would you never want played at your party or gathering?

1729. Imagine getting zapped six feet to your right—what's there, and are you okay?

1730. Is there anything you avoid or do out of pure superstition, even if you know it's silly?

1731. What nickname stuck with you the longest, and how did you earn it?

1732. What is been the best win or standout moment this month?

1733. Who was your last high-five for—sports, success, or just because?

1734. Have you ever received something at home that made you wonder who sent it—and what did you do?

1735. Which two-person act do you think could rival your own banter with your best friend?

1736. Did your dad or mom ever surprise you by knowing something you didn't tell them?

1737. If you had the chance to reset part of your routine, mindset, or environment, what would you change?

1738. What's one thing you're notoriously bad at, but your friends tease you about with love?

1739. When you return after a long day, what reminds you you're truly "home"?

1740. What's a recent debate that pushed you to speak up or reflect on your values?

1741. What's your karaoke power ballad or pump-up song that you'd own on stage?

1742. Is there a family member whose driving style is, let's say... uniquely stressful?

1743. What's the one seat at home that feels like it's built just for you?

1744. What did your mom—or someone close—always give you when you were under the weather?

1745. No towel. No time. What's your move when it's just you and a dripping floor?

1746. When was the last time you bumped into someone in an unexpected place—and what happened?

1747. What's the one movie line you keep bringing up—at the perfect (or totally random) moment?

1748. Did you ever have a long-distance pen pal growing up? Where were they from?

1749. What sneaky strategy works best when you need your dog—or kid—to take something they hate?

1750. How long would it take for someone to check on you if you went quiet at home?

1751. What reality would be too hard to face, even if you were ready for anything else?

1752. Do instant replays make the game fair—or just slow it down?

1753. What skill do you wish you learned in school that would've helped in real life?

1754. Imagine a rooster's feisty rival—what name would you give to the adventurous hen in your book?

1755. What's one "man-to-man" piece of advice that you still believe in and share?

1756. What tough, manly material would make a hilarious new version of Stonehenge?

1757. What animal print outside your tent would make you grab your gear and run?

1758. You're king of your own land. What tough-sounding name would your money have?

1759. What trend or habit do you wish guys would finally give up?

1760. If a buddy crossed a legal line, would loyalty or justice come first?

1761. Who's the last person who tried to stare you down—and who flinched first?

1762. What wild beast deserves a place in the zodiac, and what traits would it bring?

1763. When's the last time you switched your phone case to something more rugged or bold?

1764. Which goodbye—whether to a place, person, or past—left the biggest impact on you?

1765. What's the one fashion thing you saw and said, "Nope, I'm not doing that"?

1766. When you want a crystal-clear view, what's your best hack for streak-free windows?

1767. What animal name would you give a new glue brand that sticks no matter what?

1768. Which weekly program is your "do-not-disturb" moment?

1769. What's a "never" you've had to eat your words on?

1770. Who's that one guy who panics over every symptom, and what did he convince himself he had?

1771. What's the creepiest, most abandoned-looking house you've seen, and what did it remind you of?

1772. If sirens could sound cool instead of urgent, what fun sound would you pick?

1773. What's your "geek-out" topic that makes others yawn but makes your day?

1774. If you had a trainer, would you aim for strength, endurance, or just less stress?

1775. What's a bold juice blend you'd actually drink, and what would you call your signature mix?

1776. If your life were a series, what rock or rap song would play as your entrance theme?

1777. Which sports icons or bands dominated your room decor as a kid?

1778. Be honest—do you tackle blemishes head-on or let nature run its course?

1779. What's your take on what really went down during Amelia Earhart's last flight?

1780. Today, would you go with the tough-guy eyebrows or the cool shades—and why?

1781. What's your secret sound trick—classic armpit solo or another middle-school masterpiece?

1782. Is there a sound—like someone flipping book pages or a pencil on paper—that chills you out fast?

1783. Could you rattle off 5 animals starting with R faster than your friends?

1784. Where do you retreat—physically or mentally—when you need a break from pressure?

1785. Which sci-fi gadget would be a game-changer in your daily life— Jetpack? Invisibility cloak?

1786. If stuck with just one anthem for a week, which would keep your energy up?

1787. When did you last mess up and own it? What happened and how did it go?

1788. Have you met someone who carries a legendary name? Did it shape how they see themselves?

1789. What's the comfort food from your mom's kitchen you'd defend against all challengers?

1790. Can you remember the last time you threw a pillow and laughed like a kid again?

1791. If you're in full sprint mode, are you more like a cheetah, a motorcycle, or a blur?

1792. What hard-hitting or hilarious slogan would you give Google if you ran their PR?

1793. In your opinion, should we have legal options for those who are suffering beyond help?

1794. Imagine crafting a crime story—how would your villain disguise a deadly poison?

1795. Could da Vinci have hidden a deeper message in that smile? What's your take?

1796. What do you think about picking your next travel spot by throwing a dart at a map?

1797. What's a show you'd rather binge without company, and what's the appeal?

1798. Are you strategic when stacking the dishwasher, or do you just get it done fast?

1799. Do you use goggles, chill your onions, or tough it out like a champ in the kitchen?

1800. What would your desk—or brain—look like without sticky notes to track your thoughts?

1801. When did a mentor or coach express disappointment in your effort, and how did you take it?

1802. Which behind-the-scenes experience would feel like a once-in-a-lifetime moment to you?

1803. Where would you draw the line, even if you were promised more money than you've ever imagined?

1804. What would you do if you had to walk away from a major commitment at the last moment?

1805. What strange habit have you seen athletes do for good luck?

1806. Should people keep what they find, or should hidden treasures belong to everyone?

1807. What lesson hit hardest when it came not from advice, but from real life?

1808. In what ways do you feel your life is easier or harder than your parents had it at your age?

1809. If you opened your own driving school, what fun name would you put on the sign?

1810. If today you could only say one word, which one would carry your feelings best?

1811. What belief or 'life hack' did you once think you'd discovered, only to find every guy already knew it?

1812. Have you visited a museum so strange it made you question how it even got funding?

1813. Which horror soundtrack sticks with you even after the credits roll?

1814. What over-the-top costume would you create for a celebrity who wants to stay hidden while singing?

1815. What's a recent moment that completely caught you off guard, in a good or bad way?

1816. What number do you always go for in games or guessing, and do you believe it's lucky?

1817. What's your take on car eyelashes — fun expression or automotive fashion crime?

1818. From your experience or expectations, is turning forty a fresh start?

1819. What's a goal or hobby you gave up on, and how did you feel about stopping?

1820. Who do you still prefer to call rather than message — and what makes them the exception?

1821. Imagine Friends rebooted with a cast of guys you know—what names would they have?

1822. What's one powerful animal that would look hilarious if it were mouse-sized?

1823. Ever had a close call outdoors with a tick? What's your go-to method for removal?

1824. If Coca-Cola had a secret recipe only guys could guess, what would you say is in it?

1825. Do any of your buddies have epic full names—extra middle names or all the works?

1826. What classic tune did a commercial totally ruin for you?

1827. What did the guys in school do or wear that made them the cool ones back then?

1828. As you tick off life goals, do you keep adding more to the adventure list?

1829. Who do you trust to get your gear when you're not around anymore?

1830. Ever had a wish (big or small) come true when you least expected it?

1831. If you could pick any spot for an unforgettable honeymoon, where would you take your partner?

1832. What's something you keep low-key that most guys don't know about you?

1833. Are you the outer shell people see or the quiet core? Where do you think you fit in the "layers" of self?

1834. What's your ultimate "that's adorable" animal list—your top three?

1835. Do you belt out the lyrics in your car—or only when you're alone?

1836. Which hit series did you try watching but couldn't understand what the fuss was about?

1837. What object in your house would make the best improvised weapon if it came to it?

1838. If you could combine drums, guitar, and sax into a manly power-instrument, what would you call it?

1839. What's a choice you made that you'd never recommend another guy make?

1840. Have you seen any hilariously strange or badly placed road signs on your drives?

1841. When you were younger, did you create a sidekick in your mind? What would you call them today?

1842. What's a product, idea, or habit you've found recently that more guys should try?

1843. What did someone do lately that really got under your skin or threw your day off track?

1844. Which allergy—like to peanuts, bees, or even exercise—would be your worst nightmare to get?

1845. If your birthday was a solo mission, would you still mark the occasion—and how?

1846. What unusual animal and funny sound would make "Old MacDonald" a better tune for guys?

1847. If you were in charge of redesigning crosswalks, what colors would you choose to stand out and still work?

1848. What's a product, luxury, or item that just doesn't fit your life or values?

1849. How often have you moved in your life—and which place felt most like "home base"?

1850. What movie reboot was a total letdown for you as a fan of the original?

1851. Imagine life in black-and-white, with just one color showing—what color do you keep and why?

1852. When was the last time something urgent made you clock out early, and what was it?

1853. Who do you know who still types with one finger and fears software updates?

1854. What noise hits hardest when you hear it—because it means something's gone or changed?

1855. What color do you think the sky should be to make it feel more exciting or intense?

1856. If that statue could talk, what do you think is going through his head about the world?

1857. What's on your phone or laptop screen—and does it say something about who you are?

1858. What keeps you loyal to your current city or town? Name three standout features.

1859. What's your go-to move when a fly invades your man cave or living room?

1860. What's one habit a roommate could have that would drive you up the wall?

1861. You've claimed a private island—what rugged or bold name would you give it?

1862. What's your go-to reply when someone checks in, even if it's not exactly true?

1863. When you were a kid, did your parents have a special spot for discipline? How often were you in it?

1864. Which retro cooking gadget did your dad or grandpa swear by that no one uses today?

1865. What show had you watching episode after episode without hitting pause?

1866. What do you think is really buried in the famous Oak Island pit? Treasure or just legend?

1867. Are you someone who builds camaraderie fast—or does it take time to trust others?

1868. What's the strangest thing you could order online if you had some cash to burn?

1869. Tell me about a time your phone or tool went dead when you really needed it.

1870. What's something a colleague or influencer said that made you instantly skeptical?

1871. If you had the power to alter a significant moment in history, what would you change and for what reason?

1872. Which outdated workout style or gym accessory are you glad is gone?

1873. What shades represent you best when you're being 100% real?

1874. You've got a gang of cats—what's a clever naming theme you'd use to keep track of them?

1875. What flashy or over-the-top item do you think defines wealthy guys showing off?

1876. What's your most unforgettable wedgie story from school, sports, or friends?

1877. Do you catch yourself reacting before gathering the full story— especially in tough situations?

1878. What intense film becomes unintentionally funny when "die" turns into "dance"?

1879. Imagine your car is stuck in a blizzard—what survival strategy do you fall back on?

1880. Who are six famous folks you wouldn't want at your table because they'd kill the vibe?

1881. Who would you steer clear of if you had to be completely honest all day long?

1882. What kind of pasta design would you invent that pairs perfectly with meat sauce?

1883. Can you recall a time you misjudged something and had to admit your mistake?

1884. Where do you predict the global headcount will be in 50 years, and why?

1885. If you could create a giant structure shaped like anything, what would it be and why?

1886. What old TV jingle instantly takes you back in time when you hear it?

1887. What's your go-to reaction when frustration hits a boiling point?

1888. What discontinued profession from history do you think you would've nailed?

1889. Would you hike the stairs, work remotely, or find a clever workaround if the elevators broke?

1890. Would you choose a strong lion tail, a sneaky monkey one, or something entirely different?

1891. What's a cool or funny name you'd give a clownfish if you discovered one while diving?

1892. Would knowing you're being recorded at work or school make you act differently?

1893. Has the pressure to stay connected 24/7 ever interfered with your peace of mind?

1894. Which male relative do you feel understands you most, and how has that shaped you?

1895. When you're sick, what's your least favorite part of trying to push through the day?

1896. Imagine you got an award for a rock anthem—what would the song be about?

1897. What action movie was hilariously bad but fun to watch anyway?

1898. Is there a past moment you can't shake off, no matter how many years pass?

1899. What funny or unexpected sound would you add to a nursery rhyme?

1900. If you could design your ideal life location 20 years from now, where would that be?

1901. What fruity snack or drink flavor do you think is way off from the real thing?

1902. Do you consciously try to hit your daily produce goal, or is it not a priority?

1903. What practical, hands-on thing do you do regularly to lower your environmental impact?

1904. What public space would be the boldest—and coolest—place for a new Banksy piece?

1905. Was there ever a person—famous or not—whose work or courage made you proud to be a fan?

1906. Do you lean toward logical explanations or wild conspiracy theories when it comes to ghost ships?

1907. If your action-hero name was based on your pet and surname, what would it be?

1908. Which fruit do you always pick first, and does it reflect your mood or energy?

1909. Have you ever had to choose between a relationship and your professional growth?

1910. Have you ever been in a traffic jam caused by something so strange it felt unreal?

1911. What three areas of knowledge do you think are essential for navigating real life?

1912. Is there something you own that's not expensive but would be hard to replace emotionally?

1913. Are discussions about loss or grief something you've faced head-on or brushed aside?

1914. What's the most "manly" task or fix you've learned by watching a YouTuber break it down?

1915. Do you subscribe to the "rarely wash denim" theory, or do you clean them regularly?

1916. Is animal testing a necessary evil, or should we push for more humane innovations?

1917. What kind of global day would you love to put on the calendar—just for laughs or legacy?

1918. Have you ever identified strongly (or not at all) with the traits linked to your sign?

1919. Would you develop, farm, preserve, or sell a big plot of land if it landed in your lap?

1920. Which cooking gadget do you regret buying—or just never figured out how to use?

1921. Was there ever a fictional heroine you secretly thought would make the perfect partner?

1922. Would you face the unknown of a black hole like an explorer—or avoid it at all costs?

1923. As leader of a new country, what bold statement would your national flag make?

1924. What's a job you could never do—even for a lot of money—and what makes it unbearable?

1925. What's the most ridiculous or frustrating item you've ever had to chase down outdoors?

1926. What adorable animal would you never want to cross paths with in the wild?

1927. In a worst-case bathroom emergency, what's your last resort if the TP runs out?

1928. Which comedian's style—deadpan, edgy, slapstick—cracks you up the most?

1929. Is there a challenge or lifestyle choice you know without a doubt isn't for you?

1930. What's your ultimate "let's do this" anthem for a big entrance before a match?

1931. Do you twist, scoop, or cut your pasta—and does it matter to you?

1932. What are you great at that people expect you to do, even though you don't like doing it?

1933. Do you believe surveillance tech like facial recognition helps protect or over-police society?

1934. Have you ever gone horseback riding—maybe during a trip or adventure?

1935. Imagine you're sailing the seas—what's your bold, pirate-style nickname?

1936. You've got hours to kill before a flight—what's your go-to way to make the time fly?

1937. What fierce animal would make a more legendary villain than a wolf in children's stories?

1938. What kind of updates or photos do you tend to post on your socials?

1939. Is proof always necessary for you to believe in something, or do instincts matter too?

1940. If you could construct your dream cabin from anything—even wild stuff—what would it be?

1941. Can you recall a time you were absolutely freezing—was it an adventure or a mistake?

1942. Do any of your buddies have an odd or "wrong" way of eating something classic, like a KitKat?

1943. Which series would lose your attention fast if it was the only thing on repeat?

1944. Do you see yourself as typical or different from the "standard" image of someone from your country?

1945. Do you go for comfort, sound quality, or durability when picking your headphones?

1946. Have you ever had to leave a place fast because of a fire drill or real alarm? What did you do?

1947. Where did you love going as a kid—camp, the woods, the garage—and have you revisited it?

1948. What's one surprising or manly item you wish could be reused or repurposed?

1949. If you could launch a positive action in your community—what would you rally the guys to do?

1950. Have you ever come up with your own slang or nickname that should be officially recognized?

1951. Was there a time you realized doing less—or owning less— actually worked out better?

1952. Which leader or trailblazer from history would you be proud to greet in person?

1953. Imagine stepping into adventure—what rugged boots would carry you through?

1954. What's the most ridiculous or essential thing you've ever had to dig out of the trash?

1955. Do you have a guy-thing you do your own way, even if it's not the usual way?

1956. What do you think you'd struggle with the most if you had to live like it was 1985 again?

1957. What object, vehicle, or character best matches your height?

1958. Who in your circle or out in the world seems to be winning big this week?

1959. Which public figure draws the kind of followers you'd never want to be around?

1960. Do you have a go-to table when you're out with the guys? What makes that spot feel right?

1961. Is there a rule you'd bend just once if you knew it wouldn't backfire? What would you do?

1962. Have you ever found yourself humming a show tune while doing something like driving or working out? Which one?

1963. What's your favorite way to escape into nature—hiking, fishing, or just sitting outside?

1964. What food have you seen eaten in public that made you stop and think, "Really, here?"

1965. If you ran a company, how would you make your product packaging unforgettable—bold, gritty, fun?

1966. What's a chore or plan you've recently talked your way out of, and how did you pull it off?

1967. Have you ever found yourself needing to use first aid in a high-pressure situation? How prepared were you?

1968. What's the dominant thought or concern that's been following you today?

1969. Which legendary painting or sculpture would you love to have in your man cave or office, and why?

1970. Was there a show you really invested in, only for the ending to totally miss the mark?

1971. Imagine you're a music icon with just one name. What name would strike the right chord?

1972. What's a game-changing innovation you think scientists are close to making real?

1973. Is there a sports legend, actor, or musician you admire who should be honored in Hollywood?

1974. Is it tough for you to say "I'm sorry"? When does it feel most uncomfortable?

1975. What's the most unforgettable sunset you've seen—maybe after a hike or road trip?

1976. Is there a regular expense you could trim or cut to boost your savings fast?

1977. Imagine coming back as a classic item—maybe a watch, a guitar, or a car. What would reflect you?

1978. What tradition, monument, or story from your country do you feel proud of and want to protect?

1979. Was there a time when you got completely lost in a project, game, or goal and didn't notice the clock?

1980. Are there things dads or father figures sometimes do that might affect kids long-term, even if they don't mean to?

1981. What's a bold or playful name you'd give to a knock-off version of Pop-Tarts—maybe with a macho twist?

1982. Was there a decision, message, or action in the last hour you wish you'd handled another way?

1983. You open the door and it's Tom Hanks and Ozzy Osbourne—what kind of wild request do they have for you?

1984. Are you the kind of guy who can still do fast math without a calculator, or do you freeze up?

1985. Do you think arranged marriages can work for men today, or are they more about tradition than choice?

1986. Would you ever eat wild meat found on the road if it meant surviving in the wild or on a mission?

1987. What sport, band, or habit did your teenage self swear would last forever—but didn't?

1988. What's your rule for sending food back—when is it worth speaking up and when do you just eat it?

1989. Imagine a glue that doesn't stick at all—what silly or ironic name would you brand it with?

1990. In your ideal version of a candy-themed world, what snack would grow on trees—jerky branches or root beer trunks?

1991. What's the furthest point from your hometown you've ever explored, and why did you go?

1992. Is there a composer or piece of classical music that gets you into a calm or focused state?

1993. What's the next big tech gadget guys will want to have instead of phones?

1994. Would you have liked a classroom pet growing up—or would it have been more of a hassle?

1995. What experience or mindset do you wish you could bottle up and access during tough times?

1996. When has indulging too much in something you loved led to burnout or boredom?

1997. Have you ever spotted something wild being hauled down the highway—like a boat, tank, or giant statue?

1998. Which color would you sacrifice from the rainbow if one had to go—red, orange, yellow?

1999. Do you think wearing sunglasses inside is a power move, a fashion choice, or just strange?

2000. Was there ever a uniform that made you feel powerful—or awkward? What was the story behind it?

2001. Have you ever had a food combo so bad it made you rethink your choices?

2002. If you had the skills to win a global title, what would you want that title to be?

2003. What app do you keep tapping into—and does it help or distract you from your goals?

2004. Which historical or modern figure do you believe best defined strength or leadership?

2005. Is there a hat you think adds confidence—or comedy—when you wear it?

2006. What would be a strong, daring name for a racehorse you'd proudly cheer for?

2007. What's a one-liner you'd use just to throw someone off in a funny way?

2008. What kind of car would you love to own that matches your vibe—rugged, fast, or classic?

2009. If your signature pie had an unexpected twist, what bold flavor would you hide in it?

2010. Which actor do you think could bring a fresh edge to Bond's legacy?

2011. Create the name of a fierce or mischievous alien species. What's their story?

2012. What's a common stereotype or assumption people make about you that you wish you could correct?

2013. Do you have a specific strategy for cookies—bite, twist, dunk, or something else?

2014. Which sports or talk show would you love to cheer for in person as part of the audience?

2015. When was your last bus ride, and did you end up chatting with someone interesting?

2016. What bold or weird Jell-O flavor would you love to see at a party?

2017. Have you ever held onto something you learned about someone out of respect or caution?

2018. What would your breakout bestselling book be about—action, ideas, or life lessons?

2019. Are you the kind of person who follows their gut? Has it helped or misled you?

2020. What's one quirky thing you do that might make your buddies call you "crazy"?

2021. How many important numbers could you dial without looking them up—just like in the old days?

2022. Do the people closest to you joke that you have high standards for something?

2023. When was the last time you ditched the GPS and just asked a stranger for directions?

2024. What's a common belief outsiders have about your country that makes you roll your eyes?

2025. Imagine you're on a mission for adrenaline—what building or cliff are you launching from?

2026. What activity brings you peace or power that you'd love to make part of your daily routine?

2027. What's the most challenging mental riddle you've ever solved (or tried to)?

2028. Is there any clothing style that's an absolute "nope" for you?

2029. If it became mandatory to have a piercing, where would you get yours—and why?

2030. Imagine being your dog or cat for 24 hours—what would your day look like?

2031. Which commercial do you think completely missed the mark—but still stuck with you?

2032. When was the last time something small really pushed your buttons more than it should've?

2033. Who were the biggest music names of the 2000s that still get your head nodding?

2034. What's the one goal you're determined to achieve, no matter how long it takes?

2035. Imagine your liver, lungs, or heart had to be visible—what would you pick, and how would you show it off?

2036. What's one epic stage production or concert you haven't seen yet but would drop everything for?

2037. Have you ever thought about enhancing your looks surgically—or do you know someone who has?

2038. What luxury-related annoyance gets under your skin even though you know it's silly?

2039. What's something uncomfortable you did recently that pushed your limits—and what did you learn?

2040. Which TV-show kitchen looks like the kind of place you'd want to host game day or cook up something epic?

2041. If you were to grow a tree that represents your roots or strength, which kind would it be?

2042. What moment tested your grit the most—and how did you push through?

2043. Got any birthmarks or scars that have a story or just feel like your personal signature?

2044. Ever known someone who craved something wildly unexpected while expecting?

2045. Which band would you love to bring the beat for if you were their drummer for one epic show?

2046. What's the task that always sits on your to-do list a little too long?

2047. Would you want to master a cool fictional language like Elvish or Dothraki? Which one and why?

2048. What gadget, tool, or idea do you look at and think, "I could've come up with that"?

2049. Which smell takes you back to a great moment—something you'd really miss?

2050. Is there a public figure who represents a worldview or lifestyle completely different from yours?

2051. Do others tend to overestimate or underestimate your age, and do you care?

2052. Which athletic activity do you think pushes the body and mind to their peak?

2053. What fun or bold name would you give Peter Rabbit if he had a new personality?

2054. What's the most recent thing you stuck to your fridge—game schedule, takeout menu, or something else?

2055. If your first set of wheels had a name, what would it be? Something tough, funny, or cool?

2056. What's the most persistent spam email you keep getting—crypto, watches, or "bro deals"?

2057. What was the last family trip you went on—was it adventurous, restful, or a mix of both?

2058. Is there a dream job that looks amazing but you know deep down it's not your lane?

2059. You're kicking off your talk show—who's the guest that sets the tone and sparks attention?

2060. Imagine your doorbell could sound like your favorite engine— what kind of roar or rev would it make?

2061. Was there a conversation today where you wish you'd said more—or less?

2062. What everyday annoyance gets under your skin, even though you've learned to laugh it off (mostly)?

2063. If you had to dress up from a novel today, which character— warrior, wizard, or wanderer—would you pick?

2064. What's your go-to shout when you hear your voice bounce back— powerful, silly, or meaningful?

2065. What's your "I've got this" moment with home repairs—like changing a bulb or fixing a leaky tap?

2066. From a man's perspective, how does daily life or humor differ most between the UK and North America?

2067. If an alien visited Earth and spoke your language, what would you ask to understand its world better?

2068. What loud, unmistakable sound would make even a distracted guy stop and look when a truck reverses?

2069. If every night you could become a stealthy or powerful animal, which one would you be and why?

2070. What interest or habit didn't make it past this year—and why do you think you lost the spark?

2071. Be honest—what expired thing are you pretending not to notice in your fridge?

2072. When do you feel yourself getting most restless—on the road, in meetings, or somewhere else?

2073. Which track do you think will be that nostalgic "classic" you'll tell your kids about someday?

2074. If you could "save" one character from dying in any movie or novel, who would you bring back—and why?

2075. What's your proudest win from haggling—whether in a market, business deal, or big purchase?

2076. What's your personal "Achilles' heel"—the thing that always gets you, even when you're trying to stay strong?

2077. Do you have a go-to Independence Day ritual—fireworks, friends, food—or do you switch it up each year?

2078. What's your go-to way of saying you're running on empty in today's hustle culture?

2079. Who are the four men or mentors in your life you'd proudly put on a mountain?

2080. Would you have liked the freedom to choose reading material back in school? What would you have picked?

2081. Ever had to bluff or charm your way out of an embarrassing situation? What happened?

2082. In your life experience, have second chances or unexpected paths led to something big?

2083. Are you a black coffee, double espresso, or secret-menu guy— and what's the story behind it?

2084. What kind of dream would you capture in a bottle to inspire courage, and who would you give it to?

2085. What's something you've read aloud recently—whether to teach, impress, or amuse?

2086. What bold or playful name would you give your own line of guy-friendly greeting cards?

2087. Who's the most legendary athlete in your eyes—and what about their mindset or grit stands out?

2088. Have you ever been judged for doing things your own way— even when you had your reasons?

2089. Which track always gets your head nodding or foot tapping—no matter where you are?

2090. What's your ultimate sandwich combo—grilled, loaded, or classic—and when did you last enjoy it?

2091. What bold, thrilling name would you give a firework that explodes like a battle cry?

2092. What would a grumpy garden gnome be fishing for—treasure, peace, or lost tools?

2093. When would a powerful roar help you make a statement—on the field, in the office, or at home?

2094. As you gain years, what's one thing that's become more meaningful or satisfying?

2095. Do you tend to stick with "heads" or "tails" when flipping a coin—or does it depend on the moment?

2096. How do you define a fulfilling life—through achievement, legacy, or something else?

2097. What blog would you launch to express your insights, skills, or humor—and what bold name would it carry?

2098. Which public figure would be your ideal partner for a trip through a gadget or sports store?

2099. What makes a Super Bowl party feel right—wings, chili, nachos, or something from the grill?

2100. What single memory would you never trade—because it shaped who you are or who you love?

2101. What's your ultimate comfort food for watching a game, movie, or show at home?

2102. Which traditional profession do you think society has undervalued, even though it still matters?

2103. Do you mask your emotions with humor, silence, or focus? What does that look like for you?

2104. What's one phrase or inner comment that's echoed in your mind lately?

2105. Could you coach someone in tying a shoelace over the phone—no visuals, just voice?

2106. If you were decorating the tree your way, what would go on top instead of the usual star?

2107. When does gear, clothing, or tools cross over from outdated to classic in your book?

2108. What's your go-to way to reset when the pressure's building?

2109. Ever shouted at the sky on a long night just to release some steam?

2110. What's the most boring place you've ever been trapped in, and how did you kill the time?

2111. What moment makes you feel alive, clear-headed, and completely in your zone?

2112. Which key on your keyboard could you do without—and how would it change your typing?

2113. What medical procedure or test do you always try to postpone?

2114. Who earned your latest round of applause—on the field, stage, or screen?

2115. Have you ever used spare change in a creative or symbolic way—other than buying something?

2116. Do you ever line up your tools or supplies in a specific order, like by color or size?

2117. What's the most bizarre thing you've ever seen or heard someone steal from a store?

2118. If you could live a day as a woman, what would you be most interested in seeing or doing?

2119. What would happen if you combined the names of two music or sports legends—what would the result be?

2120. What class gave you the hardest time growing up, and did you ever totally bomb a test or assignment?

2121. What's a question that hits too close to home and you'd rather not answer in public?

2122. Have you ever stood near a huge waterfall and felt its power up close? Where was it?

2123. What's an old-school name that no dad today would likely give to his son?

2124. Do you remember ever checking under your bed growing up—or maybe even recently?

2125. What baby animal do you think is so cute it could stop a tough day in its tracks?

2126. What piece of clothing do you wish guys would stop wearing altogether?

2127. What ridiculous sound should come out of a car horn to make people laugh instead of yell?

2128. What was the most epic birthday cake you ever had, and how old were you?

2129. Who's a celebrity you bet acts totally different and probably boring off-stage?

2130. When was the last time you put on your sharpest outfit, and what did it say about your confidence?

2131. What Christmas movie do you end up rewatching every year, even if you've memorized the lines?

2132. What's the one thing you're determined to tick off your list before the day ends?

2133. Imagine being a black belt—you get one dramatic karate chop. What are you breaking?

2134. What's the one instrument that, if you could master it, would boost your cool factor overnight?

2135. What's the most recent situation that pushed you out of your comfort zone or tested your confidence?

2136. What's the toughest or crunchiest food that's ever made you regret taking a bite?

2137. If you had grown up somewhere adventurous—like a jungle or mountain village—where would it be?

2138. What word do people mispronounce that always gets under your skin or cracks you up?

2139. Which body part would be most convenient to detach during a tough workout or long meeting?

2140. In a dire situation, would you part with a body part to support your family?

2141. What product aligns with your vibe so much that you'd happily be its spokesperson?

2142. What's the claim to fame in the place where you grew up—sports, food, people, or something else?

2143. You're in charge of a tough, cool new boy band. What would you name the group?

2144. When do you think a man is most prepared to build a life with someone long-term?

2145. What's a moment when your readiness turned out to be a day early (or late)?

2146. Is there a blockbuster movie all your friends have seen but you just never got around to?

2147. If dogs or cats picked names for their humans, what do you think they'd choose?

2148. What "scientific" or "common sense" idea do you suspect is completely wrong?

2149. When do you feel it's right to give up your spot for someone else in a packed space?

2150. What's the last jaw-dropping thing you saw, whether shocking or amazing?

2151. Is there a "guy way" you eat your favorite candy, like biting or peeling it?

2152. If you could toss a message into the ocean for someone to find, what would it say?

2153. What action would you add to "If You're Happy and You Know It"—something unexpected and fun?

2154. When did you last treat yourself to your ultimate comfort meal?

2155. If your life was a show, what kind of wingman or backup would you want on screen?

2156. How do you imagine the most relaxing Sunday—with no pressure and all your favorite things?

2157. Are there topics you'd rather not dig into because the answers might shake things up?

2158. Have you come across any data or number that totally blew your mind?

2159. Have you ever made a quick call about someone that turned out to be completely off?

2160. What part of your body do you absolutely need to defend when the tickling starts?

2161. What kind of statue would you build to leave your mark in your community?

2162. Do you believe in warning signs—like cracked mirrors or black cats—and why?

2163. Which elemental sign are you, and do you think it says anything true about your personality?

2164. What film got spoiled before you saw it, and did it ruin the experience?

2165. How do you boost a friend's mood when they've had a rough day?

2166. What pieces of advice or values from your mother still shape your actions today?

2167. Imagine needing help to eat—what food would make you cringe if it was on the menu?

2168. What's your no-swear reaction when you stub your toe or hit your elbow?

2169. Who's the guy you know who's done great things but never brags about them?

2170. If you could shift into three different creatures or machines, what would you pick and what would they help you do?

2171. What were your favorite competitive or active games on the schoolyard?

2172. What beach setting stands out in your memory as a place you truly felt at peace or awe-struck?

2173. Besides watches and mountains, what do you associate with Switzerland's strengths or values?

2174. Would you support changing flight pricing if total weight—including passengers—was factored in?

2175. Who's the fictional bad guy you'd least want to face in real life—and why?

2176. What's a silent code among men that rarely gets talked about but still gets followed?

2177. Imagine a post-workout rainstorm that refreshes you—what would it taste like?

2178. What's a gadget, service, or mindset shift that could save you time or reduce stress?

2179. Did you return something recently that wasn't as cool or useful as you thought?

2180. What scenes or mental snapshots play behind your eyelids when you unplug for a moment?

2181. If heat and cold got a rebranding, what colors would you assign for extreme temperatures?

2182. When you think of a guy who loves the outdoors, what's the first image or activity that comes to mind?

2183. Do you remember your first cup of coffee—was it black, strong, or drowned in sugar?

2184. Have you ever put something totally illogical—like your phone in the fridge—without realizing it?

2185. If you could take three possessions into the afterlife, what gear or keepsakes would make the cut?

2186. What's a commitment you couldn't follow through on, even though you wanted to?

2187. What would you name a framing business that sounded cool, confident, and a little bold?

2188. When was the last time you were truly mad—and what pushed you to that point?

2189. Have you ever had to say no to a buddy, boss, or partner and risked upsetting them?

2190. Have you witnessed something gross or uncomfortable lately that stuck with you?

2191. If there were a 1-in-a-million risk but you could time-travel, would the adventure tempt you?

2192. Do you remember a scraped knee or dare-gone-wrong that taught you a lesson as a kid?

2193. With viral moments and social media, do you think guys today get their "fifteen minutes" more than before?

2194. How has your relationship with Christmas changed as you've grown older—or become a father, son, or friend?

2195. Who was your first real crush, and what do you remember about how you acted around them?

2196. If you could've gone to a classic rock or rap concert from the past, who would be on stage?

2197. Imagine snow came in three colors—what bold or surprising ones would match your personality?

2198. What classic kids' tune do you think would sound epic if played with drums, guitars, and screaming vocals?

2199. What place brings you a deep sense of joy—either because of memories or dreams?

2200. What's the story behind the time you went all-in—literally—with your clothes on?

2201. Where would be the most surreal or inappropriate place to hear world-changing news?

2202. How fast can you spit out that tongue-twister about the woodchuck? Let's hear it.

2203. What's a hill you're willing to die on—something others might think is odd but you stand by it?

2204. If no one could see you for 60 minutes, what mission, mischief, or memory-making moment would you choose?

2205. Is there a zoo animal you admire for its strength or survival instincts?

2206. What's a hearty, useful veggie you'd want to grow to always have on hand?

2207. What hard-earned insight from your life would you pass on to your younger self?

2208. Was there ever a time you chose practicality over brand-name pride? What did you buy?

2209. What's the most annoying or hilarious track you'd play to clear out your buddies after a long evening?

2210. Have you ever tried to downplay a physical feature to feel more confident or in control?

2211. What's the most unusual or over-the-top name you've ever heard someone give their kid?

2212. Do you have a go-to trick for making boring waits more bearable—especially at events or parks?

2213. Whose judgment would you trust to make big life decisions on your behalf—and why?

2214. At the last wedding you attended, what went according to plan—and what didn't?

2215. Is there a sport or event that's fun to observe but you'd rather stay on the sidelines?

2216. If you ever needed someone to vouch for you—no questions asked—who's your go-to?

2217. Is there a book that changed how you think—one you'd recommend to every guy at least once?

2218. Was there ever a time you went all-in on a long shot, even if others doubted you?

2219. Is there a movie that hits you right in the gut—every time you watch it?

2220. If you had to team up with one Ninja Turtle for an epic mission, who would it be?

2221. When caught outside in extreme weather, what's your gut survival move?

2222. If you were offered a fortune for your most loyal animal companion, would you consider it?

2223. Imagine having a super-powered arm or eye—what would be your first choice and why?

2224. You jump for your life—what do you hope is waiting for you beyond the wall?

2225. What's your ideal cinema seat for the best sound, screen, and snack angle?

2226. What's one time you knowingly broke the law—big or small—and what happened?

2227. What's your go-to chocolate brand when you want to treat yourself?

2228. Imagine your nose is a thousand times stronger—what place would be off-limits?

2229. What so-called "science" drives you nuts, even though people swear by it?

2230. Which man do you admire most for the way he faced challenges?

2231. Imagine the Ninja Turtles with sore backs and desk jobs—what would their lives look like?

2232. When did you last grab the stapler, and was it for something routine or random?

2233. What's one thing you know so well you'd enjoy teaching it to others?

2234. What opportunity did you let pass by that still sticks with you?

2235. Have you ever eaten somewhere with a vibe that made you do a double take?

2236. If you needed new frames, would you go for classic, bold, or sporty?

2237. What combination of events always ends in chaos in your experience?

2238. If your inbox exploded, what would be your system for figuring out what to read first?

2239. What kind of extreme BMX jump makes your jaw drop or gets your adrenaline pumping?

2240. What slang term for being drunk do you secretly enjoy using or hearing?

2241. Which iconic TV or movie couch would be your dream seat during a big game or chill night?

2242. What's a totally unexpected or funny song you'd want played at your send-off?

2243. If the DJ played the final slow song of the night, who would you ask to dance with you?

2244. Do you feel more motivated or restless after completing something big? What usually comes next?

2245. Be honest—how many inches would you have lost today if every phone check cost you one?

2246. What do you reach for to give food a kick when there's no salt or pepper in sight?

2247. Who do you know that means well but should never choose your outfit?

2248. What meme do you always share in group chats when you need a laugh?

2249. What's your personal rule when it comes to breaking something borrowed—fix, replace, or explain?

2250. What resource, habit, or value do you think men could benefit from having more of in life?

2251. Have you ever tried mastering an old-school cooking technique just for the experience?

2252. What's a phrase from your hometown that only someone from there would understand—and maybe laugh at?

2253. Where's your secret go-to hiding spot for treats or tiny treasures at home?

2254. What two questions would you ask a new friend to see what they're really about?

2255. Would you support banning the sale of ancient fossils to protect science, or should people be free to buy them?

2256. Who do you protect, lean on, or lead that makes up your personal definition of family?

2257. Outside of work, who do you spend your time with most—and how do they influence the man you are?

2258. Are you someone who needs to see things for yourself, even when told not to?

2259. Is there a bug that still gives you the chills, no matter how old you get?

2260. What's your go-to setting for a first date that balances comfort and confidence?

2261. Is there a movie where you think a different male lead could've made it more epic?

2262. Is there someone or something that always gets a grin out of you, no matter what kind of day you're having?

2263. Have you ever witnessed a guy older than you totally miss the mark despite his age?

2264. How would you react—logically or instinctively—if you came face-to-face with a bear?

2265. What's the loudest place you've ever been, and how did you handle the chaos?

2266. If a tiny but furious dog blocked your way, would you outwit it or stand your ground?

2267. Did you ever have a hiding place that was so good no one could find you?

2268. What's one rule or behavior from your childhood you've promised yourself not to repeat?

2269. What does "clean air" smell like to you—maybe after a hike, a storm, or a long drive?

2270. Do you believe hunting big game serves a purpose, or should it be banned entirely?

2271. Is there a pair of iconic boots or sneakers from a movie that you'd want to try on for a day?

2272. Is there a guy you still owe a borrowed item to—or forgot to return long ago?

2273. What's the most ridiculous nickname you've heard for a fart—and do you ever use it?

2274. What's something you'd upgrade about yourself with a snap— maybe physical, maybe mental?

2275. If you nailed a performance and won an award, what would your dance style be?

2276. What's something you dove into and then realized—this isn't worth the time or stress?

2277. Picture yourself hopping all day—what part of your routine would be nearly impossible?

2278. What practical place or service do you wish had a drive-thru window—no fuss, just function?

2279. What's a time when you laughed until you cried... or almost lost control?

2280. If someone left a mess on the sidewalk with their dog, what would you do—or want done?

2281. In a pinch, what tool or object in your pocket or bag could you use MacGyver-style to unlock something?

2282. What image comes to mind when someone says "typical Aussie guy"—and how accurate do you think it is?

2283. Where's your "just in case" drawer or place for essential stuff like passports or backup cash?

2284. Do you have a system for making sure the work at home is divided fairly—or does it get tricky?

2285. Do you have a go-to mug that feels like yours, even if it's just for coffee in silence?

2286. If you were a loyal dog or clever cat for a day, whose place would you crash at?

2287. What's the closest call you've had with an empty tank—and how did you handle it?

2288. What's a time that caught you off guard and made you feel awkward—or unexpectedly emotional?

2289. Which scene from a movie always hits you emotionally—even if you've seen it a dozen times?

2290. Imagine a fantasy world—how would your version of an elf fit into it?

2291. What two odd combos do you think make a surprisingly great team—like engine oil and grit?

2292. When a guy says "what do you listen to?" how do you sum it up—or do you avoid the question?

2293. Looking back, was there ever a time you acted tough at school and later regretted how it affected someone?

2294. Santa needs a bold, adventurous reindeer name—what would you suggest?

2295. Is there a word that always sticks with you because of its meaning or strength?

2296. What's the most frustrating thing you've ever had to rescue from the toilet?

2297. Imagine you're a candy inventor—what wild flavor combo would you bring to life?

2298. Is there a kind of weather that always puts you in a better headspace?

2299. Describe the toast shade that hits the perfect crunch-satisfaction level for you.

2300. If you earned a dollar for every time you forgot something important, how rich would you be?

2301. Would you launch into space if someone else covered the ticket— and what would make it worth it?

2302. What scent instantly makes you feel at ease or full of joy?

2303. Imagine your name was earned through a wild adventure—what was it?

2304. Is there something you enjoy that your friends might tease you for—but you love anyway?

2305. What dog breed would be hilarious to train for guard duty?

2306. If you could invent a device that helps you relax without lifting a finger, what would it do?

2307. What kind of company would you build that reflects your strengths and passions?

2308. Where do you keep the one item in your place that you'd never want broken?

2309. What's your go-to substitute when your pantry fails you during a late-night cook?

2310. What sports moment or headline recently made you shout at the screen?

2311. How would you tackle a corked bottle without the right gear—MacGyver style?

2312. What hearty meal just doesn't need cheese, even if you love it on most things?

2313. Imagine you're a daring adventurer—what invention or discovery would you proudly introduce to the world?

2314. What creative, edible upgrade would you give the classic gingerbread man's buttons?

2315. Which sport would you love to master, earning cheers from stadiums around the world?

2316. What random item did you buy that had your friends shaking their heads?

2317. Without the need to earn, what mission or project would give your life meaning?

2318. Who in your circle would turn a crossword clue into a comedy sketch instead of a solution?

2319. Have you ever stitched something out of necessity or pride—what was it?

2320. What boxed chocolate do you eat grudgingly—even though it's not your favorite?

2321. What's the most cliché place you've ever hidden your house key—and did it work?

2322. Which overused term at work or online just doesn't sit right with you?

2323. Do you go for the big chomp or the slow strategy when cracking into a crème egg?

2324. How would you calm a friend down during a panic attack—especially if they were trying to act tough?

2325. What's your strategy for loading up frozen yoghurt like a boss—layered or mixed chaos?

2326. Ever heard a phrase that perfectly captures "nerves of steel cracking"? What's your favorite?

2327. If your perfect dream had a soundtrack, characters, and a setting—what would it be?

2328. When you think of courage and loyalty—who would you risk it all for?

2329. What recent gadget or tool makes you think, "how did we ever live without this"?

2330. What bold, action-packed title would you choose if Star Wars got a reboot?

2331. Which smell hits you like a freight train of hunger—barbecue, pizza, or something else?

2332. Should leaders be given more respect—or should respect be earned no matter your title?

2333. When do you feel most grounded in the rhythm of a regular day—and does that feel like success?

2334. When everything's on the line, do you trust yourself to act—even when you're scared?

2335. What name would you pick for a kids' wear brand that's adventurous and bold?

2336. What's the loudest food you've eaten in front of a TV—and did anyone call you out?

2337. If you spotted a crime unfolding, would you jump in, call for help, or stay back?

2338. How do you react when a cold treat hits that nerve—do you power through or pause?

2339. What beast would test your limits if you had to clean up after it every day?

2340. What mutant skill would make your daily grind easier—or just way cooler?

2341. Have you ever changed a tire on your own—and how did it make you feel afterward?

2342. What's a recent time you sugar-coated something or left details out to keep peace?

2343. If you launched a magazine tomorrow, what theme or niche would you dominate?

2344. As a space explorer, what bold or humorous name would you give to a mysterious alien species?

2345. What swap between two tools or tech items would totally mess up a typical day?

2346. Do you live by the "everything in its place" rule, or do you thrive in organized chaos?

2347. If you could fix one medical problem forever, which one would you wipe off the map?

2348. Do you remember your most epic sandcastle-building session? What tools did you use?

2349. How would you explain the squishy-chewy weirdness of a mushroom to someone who's never had one?

2350. What does success look like to you—not just financially, but personally?

2351. What advice would you ask your great-grandfather if you had just one question for him?

2352. Which sports video game do you dominate, and what makes it fun for you?

2353. Have you ever told someone a different job to avoid explaining yours? Why?

2354. What small creature would be totally epic or hilarious if it were suddenly elephant-sized?

2355. What wild playground antics do you remember from your younger days?

2356. Lava's coming fast. What survival move are you pulling—MacGyver-style?

2357. What do people love to bash that you think is totally fine—or even awesome?

2358. What experiences or moments, that cost nothing, bring you the most peace or pride?

2359. When you're hungry, how does it hit you? Is it quiet, sudden, or full-on "hangry"?

2360. What hiccup fix sounded so ridiculous that you actually gave it a try?

2361. What new trend would you launch that others might think is bold or unusual?

2362. Ever practiced Spock's hand gesture? Can you do it on command or with style?

2363. If your house had a bug invasion, which one would you dread most?

2364. What's your mindset around money—aggressive, careful, or go-with-the-flow?

2365. If you had to disappear into your everyday surroundings, what would your "stealth mode" look like?

2366. You just gained the power of flight. Where are you flying to first, and what's the mission?

2367. What Disney song do you still catch yourself humming, no matter how old you get?

2368. In the epic tale of lost laundry, where do your socks really end up?

2369. What's the most awkward case of mistaken identity you've had in public?

2370. What's the most random or messy situation your finger got involved in lately?

2371. Which two legendary characters would raise the ultimate hero— or chaos agent?

2372. Is life more of a complex maze or a challenge that just needs a game plan?

2373. You're cooking the ultimate no-fuss, high-reward one-pot dish— what goes in the pot?

2374. Have you ever tweaked your age to fit in, impress, or get access to something?

2375. What line would you never cross, even in the name of loyalty or love?

2376. Can you create your own version of "roses are red"—sarcastic, sweet, or surprising?

2377. What's the funniest or most unexpected "roses are red" poem you've ever come across or created?

2378. What color fills most of your wardrobe—and does it reflect your style or comfort zone?

2379. As a kid, what did you keep hoping for from Santa that never came, no matter how good you were?

2380. You're outdoors, hungry, and fireless—how would you MacGyver a flame for the grill?

2381. If there was a dog beauty pageant, which breed would steal the spotlight for you?

2382. Whether it's a to-do list or mental trick, how do you keep from dropping the ball?

2383. You're in a building when the shaking starts—what's your instinctive plan of action?

2384. What color would you add to a rainbow to make it feel more powerful or bold?

2385. What essentials stay on your nightstand, and do they say something about your routine or mindset?

2386. When was the last time you climbed something just because you could? What did it feel like?

2387. Who do you know that could shake the walls with their snoring—and how do you deal with it?

2388. What's the most competitive or fun card game you've played recently?

2389. In the game of Clue, which character do you think could outsmart everyone if it were real?

2390. Your last supper—what's on the plate, and what does it say about who you are?

2391. Have you ever seen someone change when they became "the boss"? What shifted in them?

2392. What moment or memory from autumn would you freeze-frame for your October calendar page?

2393. Ever given an annoying object a little push over the edge... maybe without too much regret?

2394. What gritty film or show would make a hilariously awful Broadway-style musical?

2395. Can you remember a time you told your parents a partial truth to avoid conflict?

2396. If you were stuck on a plane, which Hogwarts character would drive you nuts?

2397. What do you think are the toughest parts of growing up in today's world as a young man?

2398. Did you ever show up to a reunion feeling proud—or ready to prove something?

2399. Does the place you were raised still feel like home, or have your roots shifted?

2400. Are you the kind of person who has to test the paint just to be sure?

2401. What do you tend to think about when you can't sleep, and how do you get through those restless nights?

2402. Is there a commercial jingle from your past that still randomly plays in your head?

2403. If you could experience someone else's life from their physical point of view, whose day would you live and what would you hope to learn?

2404. Have you ever committed yourself to a skill long enough to see if deliberate practice pays off?

2405. What color pair would you never be caught dead wearing, even at a themed party?

2406. What ability do you have that others often underestimate?

2407. Would you enjoy watching a film with your shoes off, like you're on your couch?

2408. What fact challenges your understanding of how the world works?

2409. What noise means the most to you—something you'd miss if it went silent?

2410. What would your "mantra remix" of "Keep calm and carry on" look like?

2411. How would you organize spices so someone could find them without seeing?

2412. What moment or image recently made everything else fade away for a second?

2413. What creature do you secretly wish someone would round up and take away forever?

2414. What everyday things from now do you think we'll look back on with fondness?

2415. Could you confidently start a fire outdoors if you had to?

2416. What's one thing you always feel like you could use more of—no matter how much you get?

2417. Imagine a lion sounding like a duck and vice versa—which combo makes you laugh most?

2418. What's one disturbing or uncomfortable thing you've seen that you try not to think about?

2419. Your tour guide's fly is down—do you speak up, hint subtly, or ignore it?

2420. What age do you think a man starts to feel like a senior?

2421. Is there someone you trust for facts or insight—maybe someone who's always teaching you something?

2422. Which bite-sized snacks do you think are overrated or way too messy for social events?

2423. What's the longest you've kept moving on the dance floor—and what kept you going?

2424. What's the latest move you've tried on the dance floor or saw someone else pull off?

2425. If you had to describe indigo as a food, what would it taste like to you?

2426. Which parts of your job give you a real sense of purpose or accomplishment?

2427. What rugged, cool or hilarious outfit would you put on your ultimate scarecrow?

2428. Do you have a system for packing—or do you throw things together the night before?

2429. If you had to explain memes to someone unfamiliar, how would you make them understand the humor?

2430. When someone offers something "free," do you tend to wonder what's really behind it?

2431. What was the last appointment or event you showed up late to, and how did you feel about it?

2432. What food craving recently hit you hard—and did you give in?

2433. What's one burning question you'd love to ask Walt Disney about creativity or business?

2434. What's the strangest item you've ever witnessed someone toss on a BBQ grill?

2435. Could you handle the dangers or challenges if your life turned into your last game session?

2436. If you had the chance to resurrect a species using DNA, would you? Why or why not?

2437. After a long day, what's your go-to meal to order in—no questions asked?

2438. Can someone truly be bad from birth, or do their surroundings create who they become?

2439. What recent offer or situation seemed so good, you doubted it immediately?

2440. How close do you usually cut it with your gas—do you push the limits or fill up early?

2441. Is there a cartoon or animated series you secretly still love watching?

2442. Be honest—have you ever used your teeth as a tool to tear through tape or packaging?

2443. If you had to invent a lighthearted name for a dad bod or extra pounds, what would it be?

2444. If you had to impress someone using just a shoebox in a minute, what would you build?

2445. Is there a donut flavor or filling that always tempts you, no matter what?

2446. How do you react when someone gives you "helpful tips" you didn't ask for?

2447. What's a funny or clever word you've made up that should exist— and what does it mean?

2448. If you could chat with a household object, which would you pick and what would you want to know?

2449. When was the last time you got stuck with the short end of the stick? What happened?

2450. When was your last spontaneous trip or wild adventure—and where did it take you?

2451. Do you think banning headers in youth soccer helps or hurts the game?

2452. Do you know someone who's always upbeat, even when you wish they'd tone it down?

2453. What's the harshest trouble you got into growing up, and what lesson stuck with you?

2454. If you could take any car, truck, or bike for a wild spin, what would make you feel unstoppable?

2455. Was there a famous person whose death hit harder than you expected? What did they mean to you?

2456. In a moment of uncertainty, do you rely on instinct, logic, or past experience to move forward?

2457. What's a clever or surprising question that would have "ten" as the answer?

2458. Imagine if a gentle herbivore became a hunter—which one would be the most dangerous?

2459. What book first sparked your independence as a reader?

2460. If you discovered a legendary man from the past in your family line, who would you hope it was?

2461. Ever scrawled something so fast or messy that it looked like code? When did that happen?

2462. What's a bold, edgy name you'd choose for your ultimate rock band?

2463. After a decade of sleep, what's the one question you'd demand an answer to right away?

2464. What are two things you believe are better not seen—especially on the internet?

2465. What's the most embarrassing or funny gum mishap you've had?

2466. What kind of sports or games would reindeer play at the North Pole, and would Rudolph be team captain?

2467. What's the most "manly" or dramatic way the nearest round object could lead to your doom?

2468. What kind of puzzles make you feel sharp, strategic, or just plain competitive?

2469. Was your flip phone a badge of coolness or utility—and do you ever wish you still had one?

2470. What are your go-to apps that make life smoother, smarter, or just more fun?

2471. What's one time your pride took a hit and all you could think was, "get me outta here"?

2472. What kind of cargo spill would turn your drive into an unforgettable (and unpleasant) memory?

2473. If you redesigned the Hulk, what color would you give him to make him even more intense or cool?

2474. What scene would you choose for a puzzle that would take real grit to finish?

2475. What's the most frustrating time you locked yourself out of your car, garage, or locker?

2476. What's the last time you stood your ground, waited it out, and saw results?

2477. What old-school trick do you use when you're feeling off— something passed down or personal?

2478. What cereal did you devour as a kid, and do you still keep a box hidden somewhere?

2479. As a kid, what job did you think would be the coolest to have one day?

2480. If you could suddenly master a creative skill, what big project would you tackle?

2481. What's that one action—even tough guys look silly doing it?

2482. Where do you stand on the death penalty—and how has your opinion formed over time?

2483. If Bond burst in and Blofeld wasn't ready, what goofy thing might he have been doing—singing in a towel?

2484. What's your take on what happens when we die—do you lean toward science, faith, or mystery?

2485. What was your last minor injury—and did you brush it off or laugh about it later?

2486. Have you ever made up a backstory for a stranger at the gym or on your commute?

2487. What's the classic "I'm not feeling well" excuse you've used to avoid something?

2488. Imagine waking up with a trunk—who's the first friend or rival you'd aim a water blast at?

2489. What's the one tongue twister that either impresses your buddies or makes them laugh?

2490. Do you believe that doing scary things builds strength—or is it better to pick your battles?

2491. What's the strangest or most surprising thing you've seen in a gallery or museum?

2492. If a dog came at you in the park, how would you handle it—stand your ground, run, or talk it down?

2493. What mix of animals would create the ultimate combo of strength and coolness?

2494. Was there a turning point or experience that made you say, "This is what I'm meant to do"?

2495. What's one behavior in other men or people that you find hard to ignore or forgive?

2496. What's the most awkward moment you've had because you showed up over- or underdressed?

2497. Do you have a recurring dream or strange sleep story that you can't shake off?

2498. Which chore do you try to avoid until it absolutely has to be done?

2499. What's your go-to way of recharging when you're feeling drained or burnt out?

2500. Is there a lesser-known show you think guys would love if they gave it a shot?

2501. If your hometown had its own Monopoly board, what two spots would be the priciest to land on?

2502. What two words do you think your team or boss would use to sum you up?

2503. What plant do you think captures your energy—something rugged, bold, or low-maintenance?

2504. Have you ever walked out of a store because of how bad the experience was?

2505. Do you ever try to communicate with your dog or cat in their own "language"?

2506. What hangout or secret spot from your childhood do you wish you could return to today?

2507. When pressure mounts, how do you find your reset button?

2508. Back in school or among your buddies, who had the best arm for throwing stuff just for fun?

2509. Was there a hero from your boyhood stories who felt like a role model?

2510. How would you break down football to someone who thinks it's just people crashing into each other?

2511. Is there a spot you frequent that always nails your favorite dish?

2512. Which battlefield or historic event would be wildest with a raging hippo added to the mix?

2513. No pressure: Can you name three Beatles tracks in under 10 seconds?

2514. What's the best banana-based snack or meal you've ever made on the fly?

2515. Have you ever played dirty in a game or test? Did anyone call you out?

2516. What were you thinking about the last time you totally zoned out during a task?

2517. What color would give the red carpet a cooler, more unexpected vibe?

2518. Which surgery or procedure would be terrifying to wake up in the middle of?

2519. What two colors with yellow would look awesome on a car or sports gear?

2520. Have you ever caught your reflection and thought, "That doesn't look like me"?

2521. When was the last time you impressed yourself by pulling something off unexpectedly?

2522. When's the last time you yawned so much that someone else started yawning too?

2523. If your cough sounded like an explosion, horn, or engine rev, which would you choose?

2524. What color makes you feel like you're wearing someone else's style?

2525. Was there something you were warned not to touch—like tools, gear, or collectibles?

2526. Who do you think carries strength and dignity in a way that defines real beauty?

2527. Do you think physical strength or endurance gives men an edge in certain jobs?

2528. What major events in sports, politics, or culture happened the year you were born?

2529. Would you choose to be a Jedi, a bounty hunter, or someone from the dark side?

2530. Which sports or news anchor has the perfect voice—but not quite the screen presence?

2531. Be honest—are you a pull-them-off guy, or do you always untie first?

2532. Have you ever eaten something with a name so odd it made you laugh or hesitate?

2533. Would you share your charity winnings or consider it fair game for your own plans?

2534. What's a route that proves efficiency isn't everything?

2535. Do you treat others with the level of respect you demand in return?

2536. What workplace phrase makes your eyes roll every time you hear it?

2537. You're heading out for a weekend retreat—what gear do you refuse to leave behind?

2538. Have you ever found a piece of vintage tech at a garage sale worth bragging about?

2539. What trait in yourself do you think sets you apart from the crowd?

2540. If you had the power to repaint the White House, what bold color would you go for and why?

2541. How do you cool down a mouthful of lava-like food while keeping your cool in public?

2542. What emoji sums up your sense of humor?

2543. What would you have the Statue of Liberty hold if she symbolized freedom your way?

2544. What two names scream "football dad" and "college quarterback"?

2545. Would you press a giant red button just to see what happens?

2546. Do you have the willpower to eat a sugary donut without wiping your mouth?

2547. If your facial whiskers determined your safe passage, what length would be your fit check?

2548. What car makes you feel like a boss without shouting it to the world?

2549. Would you give up modern life to experience history firsthand if you couldn't come back?

2550. What tune with a person's name makes you want to turn up the volume?

2551. Do you think impact matters more than size in sports, business, or life?

2552. What strengths or quirks do you share with your father or grandfather?

2553. What locker room, man cave, or sports bar wall would you love to interview?

2554. When was the last time you just went for it, even if it wasn't logical?

2555. Was there a game, trip, or event you were really looking forward to but it got canceled?

2556. Would you support an international tournament for top-tier Fortnite players?

2557. Which "so-bad-it's-good" song still hits you right in the feels?

2558. If your buddy at work had terrible breath, how would you bring it up without being rude?

2559. What's a so-called "guy thing" that needs to stop being seen as normal?

2560. If Earth were shaped like a pyramid or cube, how would that change things?

2561. Is there a part of your day you'd gladly skip—like a boring meeting or long drive?

2562. What's the one "just for me" item you'd still bring on a rugged outdoor trip?

2563. When did you last feel like you needed an extra arm to juggle everything?

2564. What's the funniest idea you had as a kid about how babies showed up?

2565. Which jaw-dropping "truth" from Ripley's still blows your mind?

2566. If you struck it big, what would you refuse to give up—no matter what?

2567. Have you ever quit a team, club, or organization that once meant a lot?

2568. Ever had a sleepwalking story that someone had to tell you about later?

2569. Which hot meal would be totally ruined if served cold?

2570. What global event or experience made you feel like everything changed?

2571. Can you think of a time you should've said no—but didn't?

2572. Will men look or behave differently a million years from now?

2573. What's the farthest you've gone—or would go—for a collector's item or hobby gear?

2574. What brand has never let you down, and what keeps you coming back?

2575. Looking back, which company would you bet on early to change your future?

2576. Do you follow the same pattern every time you brush, or does it vary?

2577. You've saved one wish. What do you wish for that changes everything—or nothing?

2578. Have life's challenges made you stronger, or just tired?

2579. Is there an item that you'd never buy secondhand no matter the deal?

2580. Do you remember the last time you danced without caring who was watching?

2581. Which pasta reigns supreme and should be the only one left on store shelves?

2582. Which cheese do you think reflects your character—sharp, smooth, or bold?

2583. If someone had to guess your spirit animal from your habits, what would they pick?

2584. Which game show would you crush—Jeopardy, The Price Is Right, or something else?

2585. What little detail takes an experience from good to great for you?

2586. Which Acme gadget would make your day-to-day life more interesting—or dangerous?

2587. What's a book that challenged your mindset or helped you level up in life?

2588. Which kids' show do you think gave off the weirdest vibes growing up?

2589. Your label reads: Bold, Complex, Unexpected. What would yours say?

2590. If you could invent the next big thing in smart gear, what would it do?

2591. Could you resist scrolling for seven days straight, or would it drive you nuts?

2592. Which person do you look up to when you need motivation or direction?

2593. What's a red flag in casual conversations that turns you off right away?

2594. When did a person's behavior make you feel disappointed beyond repair?

2595. What's one belief or standard you'll never lower, no matter what?

2596. What "grown-up" behavior did you once laugh at but now find yourself doing?

2597. Which company would hustle hard to slap their logo on a crater first?

2598. What's the strangest food plan or restriction you've followed for fitness?

2599. Would you accept a two-hour commute if the job checked every box?

2600. In a moment of improvisation, what would you grab to draw a clean line?

2601. Were there any chores you secretly liked (or hated) doing as a kid?

2602. What extreme vehicle or gear would you use to jump the Grand Canyon—just for the thrill of it?

2603. Do you prefer restaurants that feel rustic, industrial, or sleek and upscale?

2604. What's your record for bending under the limbo bar, and did it impress anyone?

2605. What triggered the last time you walked out of a conversation or meeting?

2606. What word always makes you doubt your spelling, no matter how many times you see it?

2607. Have you ever witnessed something that made you think, "This has to be a miracle"?

2608. What word do you use instead of "awesome" when you're trying to sound cooler or funnier?

2609. Who challenges your patience the most—what habits or traits really push your buttons?

2610. If you had to market your values in a tagline, what would it say?

2611. Which everyday device would medieval folks call "sorcery" if they saw it in action?

2612. What kind of restaurant setup instantly makes you want to stay for hours?

2613. When did you last lose something important—and how long did it take to admit it?

2614. What's your life satisfaction score right now—and what would raise it?

2615. What's a mission or purpose you're set on completing, even if no one understands it?

2616. What did your parents say helped you finally fall asleep as a baby?

2617. Do you give the guy running toward the bus a break, or stick to the clock?

2618. What current limit do you think science or tech will crush in the next 50 years?

2619. What knocked you off your stride, and how did you find your rhythm again?

2620. What sky pattern grabs your attention and makes you feel alive?

2621. If your life were a novel, what title would capture your grit and chapters?

2622. Is there a law today you think restricts men's freedom unfairly, and might not exist in 50 years?

2623. Is there a particular way you make a sandwich that feels like a personal ritual?

2624. Have you ever imagined driving down a cinematic road with the windows down and your favorite song playing?

2625. What usually sways your brand loyalty when everything else is equal—trust, image, or something else?

2626. Is there something in your home that always disappears—tools, chargers, remote—but no one ever confesses?

2627. Do you remember the last time you embraced childlike joy— maybe catching snow or something equally spontaneous?

2628. Which piece of workout equipment have you actually stuck with at home, and why that one?

2629. What are your thoughts on mandatory vaccinations, especially in situations where health risks affect men's work or families?

2630. When you last made a birthday wish, was it just for fun—or did it come from something real you hope for?

2631. What solid food would drive you a little crazy to go without— especially if you couldn't chew for a week?

2632. Is there a letter you find yourself drawn to—maybe because of your name, a memory, or something personal?

2633. When someone says 'home,' what specific place or memory pops into your mind without thinking?

2634. Is there a world leader you think would be a disaster in your country—due to leadership style or values?

2635. What part did you play in your school's play, and did the spotlight feel exciting or nerve-wracking?

2636. Is there something you used to think was awesome, but it feels overhyped or played out now?

2637. Would you want a heads-up if the world were ending tomorrow—or would you rather spend your time unaware but calm?

2638. Which family tradition around the holidays do you look forward to, or maybe roll your eyes at lovingly?

2639. Have you ever rushed out the door only to realize later that something you wore didn't match at all?

2640. What's something you forgot—maybe a task or conversation—that ended up making a big impact later?

2641. If someone paid you to advertise on your bald head, what type of message would you refuse to be linked to?

2642. Have you ever danced along to 'Baby Shark'—even if just to make a child laugh?

2643. What was your last workout or activity—was it solo, intense, playful, or something else?

2644. What reality TV show do you secretly think you'd be great on, and why that one?

2645. What's one song with a weekday in the title that makes you feel something strong or nostalgic?

2646. Is there a dessert that tastes amazing but overwhelms you after one piece—maybe a super rich cake?

2647. Have you ever stayed silent while someone else took the fall for something you did? What made you hold back?

2648. Did you ever deal with head lice—or know someone who tried a really odd treatment for it?

2649. What style of pizza crust hits the spot for you—classic, crispy, or comfort-food thick?

2650. If you were a butterfly, what bold or quiet colors would your wings show—and why?

2651. Was there a cat video that made you laugh out loud—what was happening in it?

2652. Do you know how to greet or say farewell in another language—maybe from travel, friends, or TV?

2653. What's the strangest preserved animal display you've ever seen or heard about?

2654. Which pen color do you feel most comfortable writing with—and why does it suit you?

2655. Which daily chore would be ridiculous or even unbearable to do in extreme slow motion?

2656. When you lost your voice, how did you manage to talk to others or express what you needed?

2657. Is there a landscape that always makes you feel grounded or inspired when you see it?

2658. Do you feel more relaxed or rebellious when you color inside or outside the lines?

2659. Is it confidence, posture, handshake, or something else that you notice when meeting another guy?

2660. When you're feeling alone, is there a friend or brother-type person you'd call to hang out?

2661. What's the last thing you jotted down by hand—notes, a to-do list, a message?

2662. Did you ever try burying a buddy in sand for fun—how long did they last under there?

2663. Imagine a storm with red, blue, or green rain—what color would feel powerful or meaningful to you?

2664. What part of growing older worries you—loss of strength, freedom, purpose?

2665. Imagine someone completely wrong for James Bond—who comes to mind, and why?

2666. Was there an anime series you followed closely—action-packed, emotional, or nostalgic?

2667. What slang word do you use for cash—bucks, dough, cheddar—or something else?

2668. Did you ever act like you knew about a movie, band, or sport just to seem cool around the guys?

2669. Could you turn empty egg cartons into something useful or clever—what would it be?

2670. In your experience, is proof more powerful than words when it comes to trust or truth?

2671. What's the one hit song that always gets you to dance—and you know it move for move?

2672. Do you remember bouncing on a space hopper as a kid—or trying it again for laughs as an adult?

2673. If you were guaranteed survival, what risky adventure would you take—skydiving, racing, or something wild?

2674. What's your go-to audio choice during workouts—music that pumps you up, a podcast, or total silence?

2675. When do you notice your perfectionist side come out—at work, in hobbies, or relationships?

2676. What cool or funny name would you invent for mashed potatoes if you had to serve them at a BBQ?

2677. Did you ever pretend to be a buddy, boss, or stranger when answering the phone—what happened?

2678. Which kind of snake—venomous or massive—do you find most terrifying and why?

2679. In a loud or packed space, how do you usually get someone's attention—wave, whistle, or something else?

2680. If you had to sum up your parents in just three words, what would they be—and why those?

2681. Have you ever had to wait forever in a doctor's office or shop—how did you stay sane?

2682. What's something that seems normal or universal, but you've just never experienced?

2683. What kind of cake would you crown king of all cakes if only one could stay?

2684. What's one non-negotiable in a job offer—something that makes you immediately say no?

2685. Was there a recent moment when you spotted something through a window and thought, "I want that"?

2686. Do you stick to a schedule when it comes to meals—or eat whenever you feel like it?

2687. What's the most impressive thing you've seen in a park—was it a skate ramp, sports area, or something else?

2688. If you were a cat for a day, where would your ideal chill-out zone be?

2689. What fear stays in the back of your mind, even if you don't often admit it?

2690. How far off the ground would you feel brave standing without any protection?

2691. What's a clever or funny nickname you'd give to tiny octopuses?

2692. What's the most recent moment when you figured something out and felt proud or surprised?

2693. What's a backup career that feels like a good fit, even if it's not your main goal?

2694. What ridiculous image or creature would be the perfect stand-in for 'pigs flying'?

2695. Was there a time you hurt someone emotionally, even if unintentionally—what happened?

2696. Is there a go-to paper plane design you swear by for speed or distance?

2697. What animal sounds can you mimic well—and do you ever use them to amuse or surprise others?

2698. Is there something you just can't accept or adjust to, even though others seem fine with it?

2699. If you've ever considered bungee jumping, what setting would make you actually go for it?

2700. Have you experienced any 'that can't be real' coincidences lately?

2701. What's your personal record for a never-ending game of Monopoly, and who outlasted whom?

2702. Which Beatle would you most want to grab a beer or burger with—and what would you chat about?

2703. Do you remember the last time your foot or hand went numb— and how long it took to shake off?

2704. Do you think about a door you didn't walk through that might have changed your path?

2705. Can you remember the craziest hat you've ever spotted—where was it and what did it look like?

2706. What sound effect would you choose to play with every step you take—dramatic, silly, or smooth?

2707. What vintage or classic men's style would you proudly rock today if it made a comeback?

2708. When do you feel the pressure to 'act like a man,' and how do you respond to that idea?

2709. What geometric shape feels powerful or familiar to you—and why do you think that is?

2710. Do you have a go-to move or skill that surprises people when you're at a party?

2711. What game world would make for an action-packed or thought-provoking show?

2712. Would you leave your info if you bumped into someone's vehicle—even if no one saw it?

2713. What's a creative or funny term you'd use to describe a loud group of little kids?

2714. When did you last take time to write your appreciation—maybe for a mentor or a gift?

2715. What celebrity have you met—or seen in person—and did they look or act like you imagined?

2716. Did you ever throw together a sandwich that sounded bad but actually tasted amazing?

2717. What visual theme or message would you highlight in a store window to really grab people's attention?

2718. Which ad from TV really left an impression—funny, clever, or just unforgettable?

2719. Is there a childhood fear that still shows up when the lights go out—what do you imagine?

2720. What herbal solutions do you rely on—passed down, discovered, or shared among men?

2721. What kind of signals or made-up handshakes did you use with your buddies growing up?

2722. What's a dream function you'd add to your remote—skip ads, order pizza, rewind life?

2723. What kind of life do you think your parallel self might be leading—and how is it different?

2724. What 21st-century comparison would you make to describe someone's strength—something techy or bold?

2725. What's the last thing you blurted out before realizing how it might land?

2726. If an 'inconvenience store' existed, what frustrating little things would stock its aisles?

2727. Have you come across anyone from Australia with the classic names like Bruce or Sheila?

2728. What's one historical date or event from school that stuck with you—maybe for how it was taught?

2729. What situation made you discover your breath-holding limit—swimming, a dare, or something else?

2730. Which interview question caught you off guard or made you really think hard before answering?

2731. Would you take it, report it, or do something else if you found a large sum of money by accident?

2732. What everyday items or rituals do you secretly love—no matter how small or simple?

2733. Have you ever seen a bumper sticker that was clever, bold, or weird—and stuck with you?

2734. When was the last time you let yourself fall into the snow just for fun and made a snow angel?

2735. What rise-from-nothing tale do you admire most—who beat the odds and why does it matter to you?

2736. When you're thinking privately, what language do your inner thoughts tend to use—and why?

2737. If you had to rename Frodo with a name that sounds strong yet humble, what would it be?

2738. Do you remember the last time you had to wear rain boots— maybe for work, hiking, or just splashing through mud?

2739. If a picnic with childhood toys happened, which sentimental teddy or figure would you bring along?

2740. Is there a phrase young people use that makes you laugh, raise your eyebrows, or look it up secretly?

2741. Would you eat something off the floor if it dropped quickly—or is it always a hard no?

2742. What kind of humorous or helpful sign would you post on the highway to reflect real experiences?

2743. Would you power through dinner if your appetizer included a surprise insect—or ask for the check?

2744. Who's the loudest person you hang around—always heard before they're seen?

2745. What cool or creative sound would make breakfast more exciting when toast pops up?

2746. When have you paused mid-routine and questioned the bigger picture—what were you feeling?

2747. As a caped crusader, what color would suit your vibe—bold, stealthy, or something in between?

2748. Which word did you last look up—maybe in a book, conversation, or something online?

2749. At what age did you leave home—and looking back, was it the right time?

2750. Which gadget gave you trouble—until the classic restart trick saved the day?

2751. What's the most thoughtful or sneaky surprise party you've pulled off for a friend or loved one?

2752. What's the one thing you'd never walk away from, no matter how tough the journey gets?

2753. You're alone, locked in the bathroom, and a snake shows up—what's your survival plan?

2754. What bold or playful name would you invent for peanut butter if it hit the market today?

2755. What would be your go-to recipe as a chef in the spotlight—something bold, simple, or nostalgic?

2756. What vanished species would you want to see with your own eyes—and why that one?

2757. Where were you headed during your longest-ever flight, and how did you manage the time?

2758. What was the big thing everyone was obsessed with on the playground when you were young?

2759. Imagine discovering a secret hallway in your house—what dream location would it connect to?

2760. Do you find yourself choosing the straightforward path—even when something tougher might be more rewarding?

2761. Have you found a nutritious version of a favorite food that tastes just as good—or better?

2762. If your pants gave out in public, what's your go-to move to keep them secure until you get home?

2763. What unexpected dream, noise, or thought made you sit up in bed recently?

2764. What current names or job titles would you give to Thomas the Tank Engine and his crew?

2765. What was the first sleight of hand you pulled off with a deck of cards?

2766. How many seconds of loading does it take before you throw in the towel and refresh or leave?

2767. Which Indian dish is your go-to comfort or flavor-packed favorite when dining out?

2768. What would you do if you stumbled across a lost ring that looked meaningful—keep it, post it, report it?

2769. Which pickled food do you reach for—spicy jalapeños, old-school cucumbers, or something else?

2770. What kind of pet have you taken care of for someone—easygoing or unexpectedly wild?

2771. What clever or cheeky nickname would you give to the little nook in your elbow?

2772. When's the most recent time gravity got the best of you—and how did you recover?

2773. What historical or modern mystery would you love to crack wide open?

2774. What would you picture counting to distract yourself when falling asleep—cars, stars, or fantasy items?

2775. What daring or stylish outfit would you rock if you wanted all eyes on you at a big event?

2776. What did your last to-do or reminder list include—and did you get through it?

2777. What would be the dream find if you dug up a long-lost chest beneath your garden?

2778. What's your best guess for how glue stays inside the tube without getting stuck?

2779. When would being ambidextrous help you out—sports, tools, or quick fixes?

2780. Which royal figure intrigues you the most—and what would you ask if you met them?

2781. What belongs on your personal "never-ever" list—something you're sure isn't for you?

2782. What made-up word would you use to describe a big, buzzing group of teenagers?

2783. What piece of clothing did you double up on but leave one hanging in your closet?

2784. With your first bit of hard-earned cash, what did you treat yourself to?

2785. What's your vision of life on another planet—strange, beautiful, or familiar?

2786. What's your must-have topping or combo when you're at a salad bar?

2787. What's the coolest multi-tool or combo gadget you've come across—like a flashlight pen or beyond?

2788. What's the boldest or most powerful graffiti you've seen in person—and why did it stick with you?

2789. Which yo-yo move did you master—or were you the type to give it one swing and walk away?

2790. What skill or hobby did you quickly realize wasn't your strong suit?

2791. What's your trademark look or stance when someone snaps your photo?

2792. What was your intro to alcohol like—and did it come with a celebration or a cringe?

2793. Got a go-to fun fact that you love to drop into conversations— what is it?

2794. Is there a childhood habit or adventure you look back on and think, 'never again'?

2795. What daring snowboarding stunt would you be famous for if you ruled the slopes?

2796. Where were you the last time you caught the sky waking up—and what brought you there that early?

2797. What rock song do you think would be hilariously great if four guys in suits sang it a cappella?

2798. What's the most you've ever collected in coins—and did you actually roll and deposit them?

2799. Have you ever acted like you had it all under control until you figured things out?

2800. Have you heard of a contest that made you laugh or wonder who signed up for it?

2801. What idea or escape filled your thoughts during your last quiet moment?

2802. When's the last time you kicked up into an underwater handstand—pool, lake, or ocean?

2803. If you could live like a monkey for a day, what would be the highlight—freedom, mischief, or trees?

2804. What landed you in hot water most recently, and how did you handle it?

2805. Were you ever the proud (or overwhelmed) owner of a pixelated pet on a keychain?

2806. What was your 'uh-oh' moment with your folks the first time a bad word slipped out?

2807. In the narrative of your life, who's been the main force working against your goals?

2808. What's your usual morning ritual—and how do you handle it when things throw you off?

2809. What local gem—person, place, or vibe—would be hardest to leave behind?

2810. Can you name a clever palindrome that stuck with you over the years?

2811. Do you believe war has ever achieved something meaningful—or is it always destruction?

2812. What wild object or vehicle would you choose to make the most unforgettable ocean crossing?

2813. What would be your perfect CB radio handle—tough, funny, or mysterious?

2814. What three websites do you keep going back to, no matter the day or mood?

2815. Do you pride yourself on figuring out the twist in a mystery before everyone else?

2816. Has something you witnessed lately helped you feel hopeful about the world?

2817. What name would you give a fifth Ninja Turtle—something bold, funny, or powerful?

2818. What horror film first tested your nerves—and how old were you?

2819. Without cats online, what animal or trend would become the next big internet obsession?

2820. What do you think would be the hardest part of immortality—loneliness, boredom, or something else?

2821. What stands out most from your school days—freedom, stress, friendship, or something else?

2822. What piece of clothing have you kept, but never reach for anymore?

2823. What animal would make the least exciting companion in your opinion?

2824. Who's the oldest person you know, and what stories or wisdom have they shared with you?

2825. What fashion choice do you think stands the test of time, no matter the era?

2826. When (if ever) did you use that line—and what reaction did it get?

2827. What movie did you last revisit on DVD—and did it feel nostalgic or outdated?

2828. Which part of your routine would be the hardest if you had stiff, unbending knees?

2829. What one wish would you ask your magical godmother to grant that would shift your world?

2830. When you had to step up because help wasn't coming, how did you take charge?

2831. At what temperature do you tap out and head for the AC or shade?

2832. What item regularly claimed your childhood savings—candy, games, or something else?

2833. Do you stick to a bed-making routine, or let the covers pile up now and then?

2834. Picture the Hulk behind the wheel—what ridiculous ride would make you laugh out loud?

2835. What flavor would you rather taste every morning than mint when brushing your teeth?

2836. When's the last time you stood in a crowd but felt like no one really saw you?

2837. What movie introduced you to the big screen—and did it leave a lasting impression?

2838. What's your most memorable camping trip—and what made it unforgettable?

2839. What tune would make guests raise eyebrows if it played during a couple's first dance?

2840. What would you decorate your hot air balloon with to turn heads or spark smiles?

2841. What's your favorite way to enjoy orange flavor—drink, dessert, or something else?

2842. Have you ever had to perform CPR—or thought seriously about learning it?

2843. When did you last step into unfamiliar territory and try something totally new?

2844. What long-distance walk challenged or inspired you most—and how far was it?

2845. What occasion felt like it would never end because of how uneventful it was?

2846. What jobs would you assign to your one-day assistant so you could enjoy your time?

2847. What's the most ridiculous or unwanted item you could imagine receiving as a prize?

2848. What's a major blunder you've kept under wraps... until now?

2849. What horrible scent would make you want to throw the sticker across the room?

2850. If I said "don't imagine something ridiculous"—what's the first image that shows up?

2851. Is there something tomorrow that you're looking forward to—big or small?

2852. Is there a symbol or face you avoid using because it doesn't match your style or humor?

2853. If you had another round at life, what being or creature would you hope to come back as?

2854. Which family member do you turn to most often for connection or support?

2855. What dish would you request from your own personal chef—comforting, daring, or nostalgic?

2856. What top three characteristics earn your respect in someone who leads a team?

2857. Have you ever caught yourself repeating a pattern you swore you'd outgrown?

2858. Do you remember your priciest pair of kicks—and what made them special or worth the splurge?

2859. What's your best guess at how many stacked chips you could fit in your mouth all at once?

2860. In the film of your life, what kind of part would Keanu Reeves take on—hero, guide, or surprise twist?

2861. Has a bad commercial ever made you stop buying something out of sheer annoyance?

2862. What's a life experience or struggle you believe no one deserves to go through?

2863. What survival gear, secret stash, or personal treasures would you pack into your hidden bunker?

2864. When was the most recent time you found yourself standing somewhere thinking, "Why am I here?"

2865. If you had to keep food in your pocket, what's the last thing you'd want to find there later?

2866. What item do you keep to yourself, even if someone close to you asked to borrow it?

2867. What innovation or finding would you want the world to know your name for?

2868. What tips the scale when you're stuck between two sweet cravings you adore?

2869. What location is a total no-go for you, no matter how incredible the opportunity?

2870. What lesson, insight, or fact stood out to you today?

2871. With unlimited time and bricks, what grand Lego creation would you design?

2872. What's the earliest joke you can recall telling—was it cheesy, clever, or cringe?

2873. Did you ever meet a real-life Karen who totally didn't fit the meme?

2874. What's your go-to app or platform when you want to soundtrack your day?

2875. If something went wrong and you had to go to the ER, who would you trust to go with you?

2876. What's the first word that comes to mind when you think of your room growing up?

2877. Did you ever collect tadpoles or tiny creatures in jars as a childhood curiosity?

2878. Have you ever checked out at the grocery store and thought, "This is a weird combo"?

2879. What kind of treat, deal, or habit do you find nearly impossible to resist?

2880. Looking back, what was the cheekiest or boldest thing you did as a kid?

2881. How many minutes do you swear by for soft, medium, or hard-boiled egg perfection?

2882. If you could instantly learn a practical DIY ability, what would it be and why?

2883. Who around you seems a bit too mysterious—what makes you wonder if they're hiding something?

2884. What style or look do you think will be laughed at when people look back on photos?

2885. Have you ever braved the rain without cover—completely drenched but with a story to tell?

2886. What three letters do you think your keyboard sees the most action from?

2887. Which actor seems to always star in films that just don't click for you?

2888. When you woke up this morning, what was the very first thing you noticed or felt?

2889. What would you do if you could walk in a loved one's shoes for 24 hours?

2890. Where would you build the ultimate hangout zone just for yourself—and what would it include?

2891. As a daring entertainer, what unexpected objects would you juggle to wow the crowd?

2892. When was the last time you watched a thunderstorm unfold— were you indoors or out?

2893. What would you carry if the undead were roaming the streets and you needed protection?

2894. Which part of your personality do you hope stands out the most to others?

2895. What challenges or surprises would humans have faced if dinosaurs were still around?

2896. When you're browsing YouTube, what category or theme pulls you in the most?

2897. Have you ever owned or borrowed a classic Walkman—and what memories do you have of it?

2898. Has anything you heard lately made you stop and say, "Wait, what?!"?

2899. With feline reflexes and balance, what activities would you finally try fearlessly?

2900. What passion did your parents dismiss as temporary, but you've proudly held on to?

2901. Has public speaking ever rattled you—or have you learned to handle it with confidence?

2902. What city or view would make the perfect rooftop for you to sit, reflect, and watch people?

2903. What happened the last time you were physically sick—and how did you deal with it?

2904. What mix of freedom, adventure, or comfort makes a day feel perfect to you?

2905. Using your three closest guys' names, what catchy band name could you come up with?

2906. Which Mexican meal do you crave most—bold in flavor or rich in memories?

2907. If you could mold your form however you wanted, would you change it—or keep it as is?

2908. Who stands out as the most disrespectful person you've dealt with—and why?

2909. Do you remember the first time you picked up a controller—what game was it?

2910. With Rapunzel-length hair, how would you keep it stylish or make it work for you?

2911. What ridiculous pair would make a grown-up version of the egg-and-spoon race unforgettable?

2912. What's the most memorable laundry mishap you've had with shrinking clothes?

2913. When's the last time you felt like you got the short end of the stick?

2914. Would you feel torn if two little ones needed homes—but you could only take one?

2915. Have you ever read about or experienced a coincidence that gave you chills?

2916. Are you the type to dive into the legal text, or do you skim and sign off?

2917. What modern metaphor could replace 'black sheep' to describe the family rebel?

2918. Do you have a childhood memory of getting busted for picking your nose in public?

2919. What imaginary creature would make a rug so odd or silly that guests would laugh?

2920. When you try speaking in rhyme, does it feel fun or forced after a while?

2921. What would your autobiography's blurb highlight about your journey so far?

2922. What nickname would you give to a sixth Spice Girl—something bold or hilarious?

2923. What's your favorite meat-free meal that's both filling and flavorful?

2924. Did you ever pull into an accessible parking spot and then regret it?

2925. What health condition do you fear the most being told you have?

2926. Would you lean into the fun of twin fashion, or give them separate identities?

2927. How would you modify a thrill ride to make it even more unforgettable?

2928. Who in your life makes cooking look more like comedy with their shortcuts?

2929. When did you last take the stairs on purpose—for exercise or principle?

2930. Do you find it easy to be direct and honest, or do you soften your words often?

2931. What random thought surprised you during your last moment of quiet under running water?

2932. What bold or surprising act would you take on in a circus lineup?

2933. Which relative just can't seem to figure out how to use technology—even with help?

2934. What's a rule you once bent or ignored, and did it backfire?

2935. What's the worst substance or item someone might regret using in a toilet emergency?

2936. If stuck in an unthinkable survival crisis, could you see yourself considering cannibalism?

2937. Is there something that once scared you deeply but now barely fazes you?

2938. What's the most ridiculous 'it could go either way' situation you've ever played with?

2939. Is there a pet peeve or trend that stirs up way too much drama in your opinion?

2940. If you were served on a plate, what gourmet-style description would capture your essence?

2941. Have you ever had something totally gross or sticky stuck to your shoe in public?

2942. When did you last do something and immediately think, "That was dumb"?

2943. Imagine you're packing light with only a stick and a cloth—what would you take?

2944. Do you have a structured system when you bathe—or go with the flow?

2945. Do you remember an ice carving that made you stop and stare in awe?

2946. What word do you tend to avoid because it just won't come out right?

2947. What's the most significant decision you've made in the past few months?

2948. How much time do you give yourself to get up and get moving on a workday?

2949. Which fruits or veggies do you never eat without peeling first?

2950. How would you handle discovering unclaimed money on a bus seat?

2951. What's the most convincing imitation you've ever come across?

2952. What's the longest you've waited for something that truly paid off?

2953. You're swimming, and suddenly your suit's gone—what's your exit plan?

2954. What's the last book that held your attention—and what score would you give it?

2955. What was your go-to face paint choice at fairs or parties when you were little?

2956. What recent moment or decision left you with a twinge of guilt?

2957. Do you have a longtime favorite piece of clothing you still use today?

2958. What pet reunion tale moved you—or gave you hope in unlikely chances?

2959. No cups? No problem. What item would you improvise to hold a warm drink?

2960. What minor thing finally made you snap or take action?

2961. Have you witnessed the moon block out the sun—and where were you when it happened?

2962. What's your action plan if a wild raccoon shows up where you least expect it—your kitchen?

2963. What were you sweeping the last time you put a broom to work around the house?

2964. What's the first word that comes to mind when you think of your mother?

2965. What platforms have you stuck with—or swapped—for your online connections?

2966. What's a home ritual you do without thinking that might raise eyebrows for others?

2967. What's your most awkward or funny wrong-recipient moment in messaging?

2968. What fictional household would be a total nightmare to join?

2969. When in your life were you most influenced by the people around you?

2970. What steps would you take if you suddenly heard sirens or alerts about a tornado?

2971. Where were you headed the last time you rode a train—and how was the ride?

2972. What's a pair of names that would make a gritty or hilarious buddy-cop duo?

2973. If you had your own garden, what plants or flowers would be must-haves for you?

2974. When you make tea, how long do you let it steep to hit the sweet spot?

2975. What moment or figure in history would you honor with a special coin design?

2976. Is there a go-to sleep position you always return to—and does it bring comfort?

2977. What's the most ridiculous or pointless app you've ever downloaded or heard about?

2978. When did you last look at someone else's life and feel a twinge of jealousy?

2979. What's one thing you'd want a lifetime supply of that would truly make life easier—or cooler?

2980. How would you spend one bonus hour every day—productivity, fun, or peace?

2981. What funny or sweet foods do you picture teddy bears nibbling on at a picnic?

2982. What's the most embarrassing thing you've ever broken while shopping?

2983. Is there a worry you carry that people close to you tend to dismiss?

2984. Imagine being a dog—do you think you'd be the record-setter for most tennis balls held?

2985. What discussion this week kept your mind spinning long after the conversation ended?

2986. Which movie would turn into a total comedy if its title ended with "versus zombies"?

2987. What's your personal best time or strategy for solving a Rubik's Cube—if you've tried it?

2988. When was the last time you apologized and someone gave you grace?

2989. What four names would you choose for a matching but unique set of siblings?

2990. What's a dish that feels like a cliché—but also a classic—when it comes to American cuisine?

2991. Who was the strangest stranger to ever share a row with you on public transit?

2992. What issue do people in your life tend to clash over again and again?

2993. Which word always trips you up when writing or typing?

2994. What setting, surprise, or gesture would turn a proposal into a love story for the ages?

2995. What trio of public figures would make for the most unforgettable (and maybe awkward) Twister match?

2996. What's something you used to love but eventually moved on from, even though it surprised you?

2997. Have you ever sensed something before it happened—how would you explain that instinct?

2998. What recent moment left you feeling misunderstood, insulted, or stung?

2999. What's your go-to thing to do outdoors when the day is made for it?

3000. What cliché advice do people give that you think might actually miss the mark?

Enjoy a Free Digital Copy of This Transformational Journal—My Gift to You

Thank you for showing up for yourself and taking this powerful step toward daily self-care, reflection, and personal growth.

As a heartfelt gift, I'm offering you a FREE digital copy of THIS IS MY WAY: 365 Positive Thoughts and Self-Care Journal.

 It's packed with inspiring messages and thought-provoking questions to help you build confidence, reduce anxiety, and reconnect with what matters most —all year long.

Claim your free e-copy by scanning this QR code:

Prefer a Physical Copy?

Many readers love having a physical copy to hold, highlight, or gift to someone special. If that sounds like you, you can grab your printed copy here:

Buy the hardcover version on Amazon by scanning this QR code:

Thank you for allowing me to be a small part of your self-care journey.

Here's to a year of reflection, growth, and positive change.

Aria Capri Publishing

www.ingramcontent.com/pod-product-compliance
Lightning Source LLC
Chambersburg PA
CBHW022051020426
42335CB00012B/635